ACCENT PIECES

Collected Writings and Moments that Decorate Our Lives

A M Y   M A N G A N

Black Rose Writing | Texas

PUBLISHED BY BLACK ROSE WRITING
www.blackrosewriting.com

Printed in the United States of America

Suggested retail price (SRP): $22.95 (Paperback); $32.95 (Hardcover)

Contents

This book is dedicated to:

Mike, Griffin and Gillian,
you are the best piece of my life.

My sisters Julie and Cindy,
your support means as much
as our love for The Hungry Bear.

Also by Amy Mangan

NON‑FICTION

This Side Up: The Road to a Renovated Life, A Memoir

ESSAYS AND COLUMNS
Salon
Better Homes and Gardens
Southern Living
Southern Accents
Thrive Global
Ocala Magazine
Ocala Star Banner
Ocala Style

Introduction

I dream of decorating. Always have. While other teenagers were fantasizing about the celebrity heartthrob of the moment, I was pining for paint chips. I get it naturally — my father was a builder who gave me my own toolbox at an early age, let me ride shotgun in his pickup truck and took me on job sites in case he needed an expert nine-year-old to help out. It's in my blood. I can't enter a room without thinking, "I wonder if this wall is load-bearing?"

Circumstance has often redefined my surroundings, but this much I know — decorating a space is a lot like decorating a life. What we choose to put inside the sacred places in our hearts leave indelible impressions. While I didn't become a builder like dad, I chose writing as my form of construction to create and honor those life-shaping moments. This is where my love of design and writing intersect, weaving glimpses of what home truly means. Over the years, I've written columns and essays about a sense of place, revealing that the best accent pieces are the ones we carry deep inside.

This collection isn't chronological and has appeared in publications over the span of many years. The themes are central to what I know and have experienced, the universal pulls and pushes of everyday life. How an unusual wedding anniversary turned out to be the most meaningful. Why a piece of china brought peace amidst chaos. And solace found in a toolbox, with faded red paint and a worn-out hammer, once owned by the man who taught me that the virtue of a really good foundation is found in structure and soul.

These are the accent pieces of my life, written with gratitude that I'm able to recognize them as exactly what they are — priceless.

HOME

I Must Be Danish

aybe it's the short winter days. Or temperatures below 50 degrees, a Floridian's version of frigid. Could be the feeling of an off-tilt universe that begs for a retreat to something less intense. Less raw in technicolor. Whatever it is, I have fully embraced the concept.

Each day after adulting — i.e. working, caring for family, functioning like a human — I often find myself in the same spot: my favorite upholstered armchair in the living room. Here's the set-up: Well-lit candles, Chet Baker Radio on Spotify, cozy robe, furry slippers, soft blanket, newspapers I didn't finish reading from the morning and Mike sitting in the armchair next to me to exchange opinions of the state of the world. Oh, and two Lhasapoos on the ottoman or one of our laps, if they deem us worthy.

The Danes call this Hygge — a "calm, comfortable time with people you love often enjoyed with good food and drinks, warm blankets and candlelight." Check, check and check! I'm a walking ad for Hygge, light on the walking part. I prefer to not see this as lazy, but fully content. Some label it with a hard-to-pronounce word with three consonants, I call it bliss.

There's another word for what ails me. I've known it since I was in high school, decorating and redecorating my bedroom while other teens were driving up and down Silver Springs Boulevard looking for fun (or trouble) on a Saturday night. I'm a bona fide homebody, defined as a "person who likes to stay at home, especially one who is perceived as unadventurous."

Well, I've had plenty of adventures and hope to have a few more, so I beg to disagree on the latter.

Yet, it's bigger than home and smaller, too. For me, it's about creating a life that is big on what matters in quiet, small ways. Take the lit candles, for example. They are everywhere in my house. I enjoy them not only for myself, but also for friends and families who visit. A flickering scented candle invites a heady combo of calm and magic. As if to say this place has been made special for you, dear friend.

Another small Hygge-ish gesture that I appreciate is actually not about home. That's not entirely true, because this is about a place that is my second home: the grocery store. I try to not be in a rush. This is hard because I can be laser-focused on getting in and out without being run over by a green-shirted Instacart shopper.

I find when I look up from the grocery list, I see my surroundings in a different way. Just this past Sunday, I ran into a friend in the vegetable aisle who had recently suffered an unexpected and tragic loss. Instead of grabbing the cauliflower and darting toward the fruit section, I stopped. We made eye contact and hugged. No words, really. Just an "I'm sorry. This sucks. I'm here for you."

It's a sad time for all of us. Kobe is the new noun for grief, a sobering reminder to live and love in the now. Times like this compel us to re-evaluate what is driving our life choices. I'd like to think we each have our Hygge moments — tiny intimacies that bring us happiness and, sometimes, to an overstuffed armchair with two puppies waiting.

I guess the homebody definition pegged me. I'm not trying to conquer the world, rather, just make the most of my Hygge corner of it. With candles. ❊

The Hope Chest

I once stored my dreams in a box.

When I was a college senior, my parents gave me a hope chest for Christmas. Once called a trousseau, the chest is a small hinged box traditionally used to hold items a woman intends to use once she is married. In other words, an outdated custom by most modern-day standards.

But, 31 years ago, the chest seemed like a good idea. Somewhat single with an uncertain future, I figured I had nothing to lose by storing a few pieces of Villeroy & Boch dessert plates, kitchenware and a Julia Child cookbook in my wooden box of wishes.

I've kept the chest though removed those long-ago items, replacing them with new trinkets and whatnot. This past weekend, I decided to take a look inside it. That's when I realized this cedar-lined trunk was never about dreams, marital or otherwise.

As the rain started to fall last Sunday afternoon, I kneeled down beside the black lacquered chest that is currently serving as a coffee table next to the Christmas tree in my living room. Opening the lid, a flood of memories poured out as if they had been securely locked away.

Furniture does this to me. A couch is not just a couch; it's the antique loveseat on which I sat to meet Mike's mother in her family room for the first time. Or the spindle-legged mahogany side table mom placed in every foyer in every home we lived in topped with a festive holiday candy dish. And the twin beds in my son's room, the same beds shared by Mike and his brother when they were little.

So, yeah, I kind of get attached to things.

And, boy, did I have a ton of things stored inside the chest. Our daughter Gilly joined me on the floor as I pulled out one item after the next.

"Oh my gosh!" was our repeated response as we looked inside our treasure trove.

Mostly, the contents were family keepsakes. A framed photo of Gilly's dance recital when she was 5 years old. Griffin's baby book. Mike's hiking agenda for his father-son North Carolina trip. The ceramic glazed horses the kids made in a summer camp pottery class. Even a couple of my "disco ball" martini stirrers I made for my 50th birthday dance party made the hope chest cut. And lots and lots of handwritten and typed family letters.

An hour later, I had created several piles of mementos on the floor. It is temporarily stored in my hallway closet, and soon I'll move the personal treasures into totes for safekeeping. Every family member will have his or her own storage container to decide later what to keep and what to discard.

For a while I was seriously channeling Marie Kondo's bestseller "The Life Changing Magic of Tidying Up." I kept more than Kondo would prefer. As I held each precious souvenir of my family's life, I time-traveled to the exact moment when that piece first existed. I was a young mom again. My son was a high school freshman. My daughter, a giddy 3-year-old discovering the ocean for the first time.

Maybe my hope chest started out as a symbol of desire, but it quickly became a repository of what my life represented, year by year, decade by decade. Yes, all those things in the chest were just things, but they were off the charts in sentimental value.

For the time being, the chest is empty, ready to be filled with something new. That, in itself, is kind of magical; the notion there's still room to add to the personal narrative, piece by piece. ❊

Paint Chip Reverie

here are certain things which give me comfort. Snuggling with my children is one of them. Watching a good movie with my husband is another. Reading a book always calms me, too. But, when I really want to unwind, I turn to Sherwin Williams. Paint, I have decided, is the ultimate de-stressor.

Many years ago, I paid $20 for a painters' color chart (referred to as the "color wheel" in the home design industry). It is one of the best purchases I have made. The color wheel has over 1300 paint samples in categories ranging from standard "essentials" like black, white and gray colors to bolder groups like "energetic brights" with vivid eye-popping hues. Upon finishing graduate school as a history major, I quickly discovered my long-term economic picture would probably not include a six-figure salary. So, paint became an inexpensive design solution as I began to decorate my first apartment. Boring white walls? Nothing that a gallon of semi-gloss can't fix. Got an old hand-me-down bedroom dresser? Slap on a coat of paint and it's a brand-new day.

Paint has seen me through some major events in my life. As a matter of fact, scanning the color wheel takes me on a sentimental sojourn. As a newlywed, I was in a real jewel-toned frame of mind with our first home. Our master bedroom was bathed in royal blue (called "Denim" on the color chart). The family room was SW 6608 Rave Red. And the guest bedroom bore forest green "Isle of Pines."

For some strange reason, I broke out of pattern and painted the dining room in a horrific shade of Pepto-Bismol pink (and to make matters worse, this was during my paint sponging phase when design sanity had completely left me). Fortunately, I live by the motto, "You can always paint over it."

Colors mark the familial milestones. There's the bright yellow for the baby's nursery, a gender-neutral color we chose not knowing if we would have a boy or girl. We had one of each over a four-year period and both used this room for their first beloved space. Seafoam green reminds me of our second home's master bedroom when we bought our first bed, thrilled to finally have a headboard. The Totally Tan paint chip takes me back when we ordered new family room furniture with matching pillows (the couches are still with us, but the pillows succumbed to years of torture by the resident pets.)

Even today, I fantasize about the next color that will grace a spot in my home. Truly, this chromatic captivation has become a visceral experience. Oh, there's probably a metaphor or two about life nestled somewhere in between the paint swatches. My color preferences have significantly changed since the unfortunate pink dining room incident. These days, I'm leaning toward soothing colors like Relaxed Khaki and Basket Beige. Even monochromatic variations of white have begun to pique my interest. Yet, hopefully, there will always be a strain of a vivid red woven in between the beige. I just gotta believe there's still a little Red Rave in my future. ❄

My Father's House

Growing up as a builder's daughter, I benefited from my father's chosen profession. Our family often rode the highs and lows of residential construction by moving from one spec house to the next. For a young girl who changed favorite colors as often as socks, I was thrilled to get a new bedroom—complete with a new color palette—every few years, oblivious to the real financial impetus for our frequent moves.

Dad also made sure I had my own toolbox. The bright red metal container held dividers full of Dad's hand-me-down screws and nails with a clunky measuring tape and rusty wooden hammer. As a child, I lugged that thing around Dad's construction site ready to help him in case his crew of 20 other men couldn't find any of their tools. Dad indulged his young apprentice, asking me to measure a window or borrowing my one and only Phillips-Head screwdriver.

Tagging along with Dad at his work site was as good and pure a life as I could imagine. I'd watch in rapt attention as he'd prepare to drive a nail into two-by-four. He was the Houdini of hammering, clenching his teeth around the smallest nail while managing to hold a hammer, pencil, and level without dropping—or swallowing—anything.

One of the best gifts Dad gave me came from scraps. After cleaning up a finished project, he used a pile of discarded doors to build my very own playhouse. The side panels were comprised of hollow-board hallway doors running horizontally, knobs intact. The roof was a mismatch of asphalt shingles. And Dad managed to salvage a bathroom sink for my faux kitchen inside. He saved the design pièce de résistance for the front entrance, placing a glass-paneled walnut door as the entryway. It looked

like Dorothy's house post-tornado from The Wizard of Oz, but I loved that place like no tomorrow.

Recently, while reading a story about a little girl who discovers an abandoned cottage, my daughter opined that she'd love to have a playhouse. Big brother chimed in agreement. A neglected potting shed in our backyard suddenly presented itself as a viable possibility. Before you could say Bob Vila, we were in the throes of a design redo.

First, we established one simple rule—no money would be spent on this project. Instead, some serious elbow grease and creative energy would shape this warped, wooden shed into a fun retreat. So, we pulled out some paint cans from the garage, grabbed a few brushes, and got busy.

After attacking the exterior, we focused on the inside, adding a miniature table and chairs from the back porch. Our dog declared instant occupancy, joining two kids and one mama hunched down in the petite space.

The children raked the area around the shed, added a few stepping stones as a playful walkway, painted in whatever color we had left. The playhouse was almost finished, save for hanging a few pictures taken from inside the "main" quarters.

Heading back to the garage, I dusted off a worn and faded metal toolbox. With the rusty wooden hammer, I returned to the newly deemed playhouse, clenching a small nail in my teeth while measuring the spot to hang our first picture. I thought of Dad. And my all-door playhouse. And my borrowed days on construction sites.

Then I told my children I hoped they'd always love this place like no tomorrow.

My Room with a View

he answering machine hummed the usual messages as I walked into our home after work and picking up the children from school. A friend had called to say hello. My sister phoned to ask me a question. Husband called to check in. Wanda Ventling from *Creative Home* called. Wait a minute. Replay that message.

"Hi, we read your entry for our magazine's porch room makeover," she said.

Then, Wanda uttered those seven words every design-loving woman wants to hear... "We are going to decorate your room."

While I am a somewhat out of shape middle-aged mother, this didn't stop me from screaming, jumping and laughing. The children ran into the room and started doing the same thing until my daughter asked me "Mama, why are we jumping up and down?"

This phone message embarked my family upon a fast-paced decorating journey that culminated in the creation of an elegant and functional sunroom. Not only has this room become our favorite space, but we have also gained a greater appreciation for the virtue of making a house a home with a little bit of creativity, vision and a lot of paint.

Through a series of email exchanges, a videotape of our home and detailed description of our porch, Wanda and her team began to see the challenge before them. We had recently moved into the home of our dreams with all the right ingredients: lots of character, good location and a great backyard for the children. However, our renovation budget didn't include the screened-in porch facing the backyard. I called it our "neglected room" and it looked like it. Old furniture that didn't find a place in the rest of the house ended up on the porch. There was no lighting and a squeaky fan hung from the ceiling.

While the rest of our home had a warm, English cottage feel, the porch looked like a cold afterthought.

In addition to structural details, Wanda inquired about our family's wants and needs for the porch. Mike wanted comfort where he could relax while looking at the backyard. I wanted overhead lighting and anything but traditional Florida wicker. All the children wanted to know was when the magazine team was coming (waiting for three weeks is a lifetime for a nine and seven-year-old).

Soon, boxes started arriving at our door and a sneak peek revealed Wanda not only listened to our requests —but exceeded them. Crates of furniture, pillows and lights lined up inside our garage. This was better than Christmas. I couldn't stop smiling. Every container held a clue to Wanda's vision for the makeover.

When the Creative Home team arrived, editor Wanda Ventling, art editor Becky Lau Ekstrand and carpenter Andy Ventling got busy. First, they surveyed the porch they had only read about and seen in photos. They tentatively placed the furniture in the room and identified where the three chandeliers would hang.

A local electrician began wiring the ceiling for the lights and contractor Brian Vachon reinforced the roof in order to support the lighting. Meanwhile, Mike and I began cleaning the porch. Admittedly, it had been awhile since I had cleaned the aluminum ceiling. Dust and cobwebs were attacked so the space would be ready for paint.

Then, Becky, Mike and I began painting the ceiling a soothing sage color while Adam and Wanda began building a sideboard. After painting a few strokes, I realized why I had always wanted to be taller... painting a ceiling is hard work! Thankfully, six-foot-one Adam helped Mike finish the rest of the painting. So, I took my brush and followed Becky and Wanda for another painting project: the dining table and sideboard.

Wanda had brought some beautiful brown transferware china that she incorporated onto the table designed by a Des Moines artist. Quickly, the room began taking shape. Two sisal rugs hugged the brick floor. A stately boxwood topiary in an ebony porcelain urn stood next to the wall. Customized brown fabric draped the sideboard with elegant china and flowers on top. Wrought iron chairs with tailored toile cushions sat next to the dining table.

What was once an eyesore became a focal point. Wanda hung weather resistant muslin and houndstooth fabric drapes on one of the screened walls, hiding an unsightly air conditioner and creating a feeling reminiscent of the 1920s Art Deco period, Hollywood style. Nearby, two patina iron garden decors were hung on the wall.

The creative coup de grâce was the customized chaises covered in an olive tapestry by Joe Ruggiero's Norwalk Collection. Silk pillows completed the seating area and a pink throw indicated which chaise belonged to me, with lush brown pillows reserving a spot for Mike. Who would have thought of a "his and hers" pair of chaises on a porch? A wrought iron chandelier graced the space between them above two nesting tables. This would be a place for some serious lounging. The other amber beaded chandeliers highlighted the painted table in the dining area.

In real life, I am a college professor, but I became a student in Design 101 during Creative Home's visit. As a teacher, I know the value of learning a

few good lessons and this experience gave me several:

Lesson #1: Paint is your friend. Don't be afraid to add some color to a room and, yes, even a ceiling. This sets the tone for a warm ambience and can be done very inexpensively.

Lesson #2: There is beauty in the unexpected. I would have never thought to place chandeliers and chaises on a porch, but the touch has added greatly to a feeling of comfort and warmth.

Lesson #3: Good design doesn't have to be expensive. As Wanda shared with me, you can choose one customized piece and accent around it with inexpensive items.

Next to the chaises are nesting tables Wanda found at a fabric store. All the fabric came from a value supercenter and many of the accessories were found in local design stores on sale.

Lesson #4: Use what you love. Wanda picked up quickly that Mike and I love traditional pieces with an Old-World feeling. All of the furniture, lighting, and fabric reflect this appreciation for all things old.

Lesson #5: Candles and flowers make a difference. On the table, store-bought roses sit inside the brown transferware beside candles in glass hurricanes. This is an easy decorating tool that allows me to change flowers according to the season. I can use clusters of red carnations for the winter holidays, pink roses for springtime and yellow daisies in the summer.

Perhaps the ultimate compliment to the Creative Home team is when friends come by to see the sunroom and comment how this space looks exactly like us. This room truly is a reflection of everything we love. Mike put it best when he said, "We are happiest when we are home." Thanks to Creative Home Magazine, we now have a beautiful room with a view. ❄

Sip and See

Glancing out the side entrance to our home, I yelled to my family—and anyone else within a five-mile radius—as the big delivery truck pulled into our driveway.

"They're here!" I shouted. "The packages have come!"

Christmas was in the air that day even though Thanksgiving was still a week away. After signing the delivery slip, I placed the two large boxes on the leather ottoman in the family room. Just looking at the packages gave me goosebumps. I was like Darrin McGavin in *The Christmas Story* movie when the lamp he'd ordered, shaped like a woman's leg, arrived in a large box on his doorstep. Tearing open the first box, I squealed at the sight in front of me.

"Oh, how beautiful," I whispered reverently as I pulled several crème-colored ceramic dishes from the plastic bubble-wrap. They were painted in a rich brown and beige design. I wasn't sure that fine china and a back porch normally went hand-in-hand from a decor perspective, but it didn't matter. Soon, everything would come together. I just knew it.

My family and I had recently moved into the two-story brick cottage at the end of an oak-lined road in Florida. Oak Lane Cottage, our family's third home, had a neglected screened-in porch with brick paver flooring and was the only one we'd ever formally named, as if our bequeathing a title to a structure guaranteed certainty. But we were sure about this house. This was the one. We had been like Goldilocks in our quest for the perfect home.

Our first place with no name had been Mike's late great Aunt Cristina's ranch-style house that had been his thirty-six-year-old bachelor pad, until his new twenty-six-year-old bride moved in. It was too small. And very late great aunt in décor with yellow shag carpet, tiny musty-smelling rooms, and 1970s-era green linoleum flooring in the kitchen, the laundry room and the family room, where it curled up at the edge of the wall exposing the concrete slab. I believe Aunt Cristina would've floored the garage with linoleum if she could have.

With the addition of Griffin and Gillian, we moved into Mike's late mother's home in a different neighborhood in a good school district. This home was bigger, but had a challenging floor plan. The master bath, which was the size of a small coat closet, opened directly into the family room with an unreliable sliding pocket door as the divider. Things got awkward when guests were over and someone used the bathroom. I would talk loudly or turn up the TV volume in the family room to drown out the sound of the toilet flushing or some flatulent noise on the other side of the sliding door. We renovated and rejuvenated as best we could, but it always felt like the home of another Mangan relative.

A half a mile away in the same neighborhood we discovered a Cape Cod-style cottage for sale at the end of a road nestled by large grand oak trees with branches that intertwined like an old lady's fingers and let the sun filter in through her canopied hands. The house had lots of potential. A large backyard with room for the kids to play. A kitchen that had good bones and was ripe for a Mangan redo. And three fireplaces! After closing at the title company, Mike and I drove straight to the house among the oaks. Holding hands, we walked in the front door where Mike proclaimed this was the house we would grow old in.

It was just right.

Well, almost right. I made a home renovation notebook of the projects I wanted to take on. Kitchen renovation. Master bath expansion. New paint for the bedrooms. Front yard landscaping. Window treatments. New paint for the dining room. Downstairs bedroom-to-library conversion. New paint for the family room. Hell, new paint for *every* room. I included a section in my notebook for the back porch update that would eventually, I knew, be the pièce de résistance of my decorating dreams.

My life became full-throttle nesting. I set out to transform this house and collected the things you collect when you say you are making a place of your own—new art for the paneled walls, lamps for the living room, and tchotchkes for tables and shelves because a house isn't a home without a brass monkey holding a candle. But our porch budget was limited, so the porch consisted of two lawn chairs.

Longing for a place to retreat, I entered a home decorating contest sponsored by *Better Homes & Gardens Creative Home*, one of the many "shelter" magazines I read. Lo and behold, I won a complete porch makeover by the magazine's very own editor, and their team flew in from Iowa and spent four days painting, building, wiring, accessorizing and furnishing my porch. Pure nesting bliss. The results featured a hand-painted dining table, two luxurious outdoor-friendly chaises with matching chenille blankets and needlepoint pillows, an antique white sideboard that I helped build, and not one but two crystal chandeliers hanging over my dining table. The wrought-iron dining chairs had custom-made tufted seating. I even had white gauze curtains hanging from each end of the porch.

Curtains. *On my porch.*

No beautifully appointed porch is complete without accessories and I had those in spades, or rather, Spode. The magazine editor had chosen a brown-and-beige theme for the porch, and she shipped in boxes of Spode china —plates, tea cups, pitchers—in a matching palette and one silver-plated metal dessert server to hold three Spode dessert plates.

The plates depicted nineteenth century scenes commissioned by a man named Spode Copeland who was rather fond of fine china and unique, long-ago landscapes. One plate had a sketch of two full-figured women lounging on an ornate Greek columned porch—kind of like my sister and I, minus the lounging and ornate part. Another plate showed two soldiers fighting to hold onto what appeared to be a pig that was clearly not cooperating with its captors.

I had never heard of brown transferware—a most unusual description of china—and yet I wondered where it had been all my life. Mike would come home that night to enjoy seeing his usually loquacious wife dumbstruck. By a plate.

An hour after Spode had come into my life by way of FedEx, I remained parked on my couch carefully unpacking the china. Gillian and Griffin joined me around the ottoman, and we yelped every time we pulled out another piece from the boxes.

"Look at this, mama!" Gillian said as she held a miniature Spode pitcher.

"Here's another one!" Griffin said while unwrapping a plate.

"We should play Christmas music," I joked as I dug into a box to pull out another treasure. The pile of bubble-wrap grew so high on our family room floor that we had to do a search and rescue mission to find our dog, Honey, who had been buried beneath it.

"Hey! Honey matches the china!" Griffin said laughing at our brown-and-white Chi-Poo who had begun jumping on the bubble-wrap as it pop-pop-popped like a firecracker. Clicking on my iPod, I found our Mangan Christmas playlist.

"Why not?" I asked aloud and began dancing around the ottoman of porcelain treasures while Bing Crosby crooned about glistening treetops and sleigh bells in the snow.

This space was the heart of our house, mainly because visitors came through the side entrance more often than the front door. We'd tell friends to come to the "second front door" when visiting. To match the brick paver floor, the room boasted a matching brick fireplace and bookshelves next to it where I kept every board game imaginable. My mom had given me a dark-stained side table that fit perfectly in between the couches and I placed a large lamp on it for ample light.

Our kitchen and back porch were connected to this space so the second front door was a direct shot to constant activity and foot traffic. And the best place for celebrations. Sometimes the party began outside the side entrance where a wooden bench had been placed next to the second front door and served as the spot to drop off packages and baseball and volleyball team jerseys.

After the makeover was complete and magazine photos had been taken, I invited friends, neighbors and family over to sip some wine and see our newly decorated porch. The magazine's makeover crew agreed to stay for the party, joking they had never been to a "sip and see," which led me to wonder if they had ever been to the South before.

In time, the silver-plated dessert server would not stay on the porch. I moved it inside where it became a running joke among friends for the many uses I had created for it. Some days the server held pastel-sprinkled mini cupcakes for birthdays. Other days it made a most convenient spot for serving bite-size appetizers after it had been given an instant promotion from the kitchen counter to the kitchen island, the epicenter of our world. Later I moved the server to my home office, a former den I had created as a place of my own to write and read, and write a little more if I was lucky. The server became my office supply accessory and held pens and pencils on one plate, paper clips on another, and a stapler on the last. The server— with its nineteenth century scenes of lounging women and escaping pigs— had a French inscription beneath the capture-the-pig painting, "Tiens Fermé," which, translated, means "Hold On." I remember noticing those words for the first time when it was Christmas in November in our side entrance room.

"What does this mean?" Gilly asked, pointing to the plate's inscription.

"I have no idea," I said, shaking my head.

Soon, however, those words would come to bear significant meaning, when the only thing I could do was hold on tight. The 2008 recession would cause both Mike and I to lose our jobs and home. Yet, we still had each other and our children. Most days, we had our sanity. And we always the most beautiful set of Spode plates to remind us that beauty often comes in grace and fine china. ❀

Scraps of Love

Once upon a time, there was a society that encouraged the recording of experience. We documented life in many ways, but none so prolific — or profitable to craft store companies — as the inimitable product called a scrapbook.

Today, these oversized keepers of photos and aged Scotch tape collect more dust than attention. However, I submit consideration of relevancy for the ancient binder beasts.

I began scrapbooking in high school. In a way, pasting photos and mementos in a book is a form of recorded history. No surprise, then, that I majored in history in graduate school.

However, I stopped scrapbooking over a decade ago when my children reached middle school. I didn't have a spare 20 hours a week to dedicate to this time-consuming hobby. Not that I ever had the time — most scrapbooking sessions took place between 10 p.m. and 1 a.m. after the kiddos went to bed.

Maybe it's just me, but it seems like scrapbooking has fallen out of popularity. I don't know anyone who spends hours culling through photos, concert ticket stubs, and recital programs.

I once belonged to a scrapbooking group of women who met weekly to stay current with "their pages." Some went on weekend retreats to tackle their scrapbooking projects. I knew I was out of my element when I didn't have my own scrapbook tool-box full of colorful borders, stickers and ink stamps.

Then again, maybe it really is just me. A quick Internet search of scrapbook trends reveals that archiving life has been taken to a new level.

Now, it's called "memory keeping," with high-tech options including one known as a hybrid digital scrapbook.

As best I can tell, this means printing personal photos from the computer to paste onto memory-keeper-worthy pages. Scrapbookers can even attend "creativation" conferences, mingle with fellow memory keepers and shop in the vendor exhibit hall until their crafting hearts are content.

Although I quit scrapbooking back when George W. Bush was president, I still have a large scrapbook collection, each album bursting at the tightly bound seam, weighing more than my dogs.

Last week, my daughter pulled one of our family scrapbooks off the shelf and summoned Mike and me to join her and the dusty book on the couch. Gilly is home for what will probably be her last summer with us before heading out of state to graduate school for the next two years followed by a one-year residency somewhere else (meaning not Ocala, Florida). So, when she wants me to be with her to look at family photos, you bet I will.

An hour later, we had laughed, cried and "awwwwwed" as we looked at each memory-bathed page.

Through the years, I've lugged these books through many home moves, often questioning my sanity in keeping them. Will the kids want them when I'm gone? Who really looks at them anyway?

Sitting on the couch that night, I remembered why I've kept them. Each album is a part of the heart and soul of my family, friendships, vacations, rites-of-passages, favorite school teachers, birthday parties and holiday celebrations.

Each page is a snapshot of how we lived. Each page says we were here and we were loved...and how mama was a saint for putting the scrapbooks together when she could have done other things, like sleep. Okay, no one will say that.

I think I should look at these albums on a regular basis as a necessary temperature check. They remind me how we only record what matters. Nary a page has a photo of an e-mail message or task list.

Back on the couch, Gilly took a picture with her phone camera of one of the scrapbook pages and sent it to her brother, Griffin. She found a photo that meant something to the two of them. I didn't ask which one. The shared memory was enough for me. ❊

THE YEARY GIRL

Love The Bear

Sometimes magic happens in the most unexpected places. Like Facebook. Ironically, the credit goes to my sister, Cindy, who still doesn't have a photo for her Facebook profile. One night we were texting our usual sister-to-sister messages (translation: cute dog stories) when I mentioned I had stopped by our favorite place earlier in the day.

"Hungry Bear?" my sister asked.

She knows me well.

Yep, I'd been to The Bear, as we regulars affectionately call it. I like to say I'm a regular at Ocala's iconic downtown drive-thru whose menu boasts burgers such as The Papa Burger, Mama Burger and, my favorite, the Baby Burger (a kinder, gentler hamburger). Like many Ocalans, I grew up with The Bear. First, I started with their peanut butter and chocolate milkshake. Later, I honed my carb skills on their spicy fries. Now that menopause has set in, robbing me of fat-burning metabolism, I try to limit myself to Hungry Bear's Diet Coke with the best crushed ice ever. From soda to shakes, The Bear can't be beat.

Except it can, unfortunately. The Bear has come upon hard times. Summer is always a tight season for the drive-thru whose customer base peaks from September to May when Osceola Middle School and Eighth Street Elementary students, parents and teachers flock for an after-school treat. June through August are the lean months as Linda Williams has often told me, just the incentive I needed to visit more often. Williams and her family have managed Hungry Bear for as long as I can remember.

But lately, a new deterrent has hit The Bear — economic prosperity, as odd as this may sound.

Downtown Ocala is thriving, with new businesses and construction projects popping up on every corner. Even one close to the drive-thru. Which means more construction, which means closed streets and access to Papa, Mama and Baby. Revenue-wise, it's like gasoline on a fire for a local business that already struggles during the summer.

Enter Cindy's brilliant idea.

"I think I'll see how many people read my Facebook messages and post if anyone wants to go to Hungry Bear, I'll pay for their milkshake," Cindy texted. "They can just ask for Cindy's special milkshake and Linda will know what it is."

Exactly, my dear Sherlock, er, Cindy!

I told her I'd post something on my page, too, but opted not to commit my sister to bankroll a pilgrimage to The Bear. Charity starts at home, people! So cough up a few dollars and partake in the deliciousness of a Mama-with-spicy-and-Cherry Coke. If you parse your order, you get it more quickly. I encouraged my friends to swing by Hungry Bear and "buy locally" as our local chamber would say.

Within minutes, I hit the "send" button to my Facebook friends.

That's when the magic happened. Or as I like to call it, the beauty of living in Ocala.

Soon, friends started commenting. Then sharing my post. Within an hour, I got more shares then anything I'd ever posted in my entire social media life. I joked to my sister that The Bear now competed for the most "Likes" as my beloved dog, Honey.

By the next day, I received reports from the field. Operation Love The Bear was working.

"I had my first spicy fries at Hungry Bear!" one Facebook friend posted.

"C'mon, everyone, join me for lunch there!" another friend commented.

Linda said folks pulled into the drive-thru referencing "the Yeary girls."

"I met some new faces today," she said smiling as she handed me my order.

Knowing our special city, I bet she'll meet even more. ❊

The Hungry Bear, Part Two

They welcomed me after a long day from school.

From a broken heart.

From college.

From work.

From the hospital with a new baby.

They greeted me with the sweetest tea and Best. Crushed. Ice. Ever.

They offered me corn nuggets with creamy insides so hot the roof of my mouth would turn numb and I was happy for the experience.

Once, I made my husband take a quick detour from a funeral procession to get five iced-cold Cherry Cokes for the passengers in our station wagon on a hot summer day.

It became my weekly pilgrimage in my thirties and emotional lifeline in my forties.

It was the place I'd bring friends who would raise a skeptical eye before biting into a hot, salted crinkle fry and pledging a lifetime vow of commitment.

It was peanut butter milkshakes.

It was the iconic drive-in with the dilapidated facade and cash-only requirement.

Linda would always ask me how I was doing and if my headaches were any better.

Danielle said my sister just came through ("Which one?").

Gladys would yell from the grill that my monthly tab was low, but not to worry, I could pay next time.

Ah, Gladys. She began as the cook in the late 1970s and eventually bought the business. She seldom missed a day of work even when she didn't feel well.

Like last month.

Linda, her sister, finally made her go to the doctor. The drive-in could manage a day without her.

Gladys died five weeks later of cancer.

Linda said Gladys worked her way through the pain. The Bear needed her.

Gladys's daughter, Angie, will keep the drive-in open, welcoming patrons after long days from school, work, funerals, broken hearts, and life in general.

Sweet tea will be our solace.

So will corn nuggets. And Baby Bear burgers. And Cherry Cokes. And Linda and Danielle and now Angie.

The Hungry Bear lives on. ❀

Dad's Boots

I'd like to officially go on record to retract an oft-repeated statement that the most important things in life aren't things, they are people. I was partially wrong. People are important, but, sometimes, there are things in our lives that rank pretty darn high. This weekend, I was reminded of this by a pair of boots. Leave it to my big sister, Cindy, to teach me this lesson.

First, you should know that Cindy is our unofficial family librarian, our own Library of Congress. She keeps the valuable stuff no one else thinks about. Like boots. More on that later.

So, before you read further, make a note of who should be your KOTTM, Keeper of Things That Matter. It doesn't have to be a relative. Any organized person who loves you will do. Not sure who? Here's a situational example: You just read *The Magic Art of Tidying Up* and decide to get rid of your vinyl record collection, family scrapbooks and birthday cards from your teenage years. Who do you call to walk you off the throw-it-in-the-trash can ledge?

Stop. Breathe. Slowly, place those items in a very big packing box and call your KOTTM. Texting is acceptable. Chances are your chosen Keeper will rush over, gather up your stuff, and walk away until you grow up and realize you really want it.

Cindy keeps things I completely forget about until I was mature enough to cherish them. Like my late Aunt Clovis's hand-written From the Kitchen of Clovis Brack recipe for field peas (hint: ham hocks make the smoky flavor), plastic bins of family photos, and my seventh-grade report card. Yikes. Scratch that last one.

Or my father's work boots.

Cindy stopped by to drop off a few things — birthday cards and gifts for my children, school pictures from her grandchildren and...Dad's boots.

If you know me, it's no secret I was one of the lucky ones who adored my father. And for good reason. He was the consummate great dad, with a DNA that was all goodness. A Greatest Generation guy, he survived World War II, economic hard times, running his own construction business, and raising four daughters, three of whom decided to get married within two years, the last of which would do in any human being. Not Dad. He loved every minute and told anyone who would listen. Some would say to him, "Gosh, Sherman, four girls? God bless you." He'd reply with a big grin, "Yep, He sure did."

At age 18, was I aware of such goodness? Mostly, no. Thankfully, my sister, who was 11 years older, sure did with the good sense to keep his things I didn't think mattered.

At early dark thirty on summer mornings when I was little, Dad would often take me to his construction site. Dressed in all denim, wearing his brown leather Dingo boots, I would hear him walking down the hallway to wake me up. "Today is your lucky day, honey," he'd say, "I need a helper at the site." I was more than willing to help, wearing my own pair of boots.

Last weekend, I guess my sister decided I was ready to be the owner of Dad's boots. There they were — the tips worn from his construction days. For once, I was rendered speechless. After Cindy left, I placed Dad's boots on my office table, which is where they have remained.

I texted my husband, sisters, and children, asking them what things reminded them of me? Paint chips, framed holiday cards, Papa's red toolbox, and a label maker were their replies. I sound like a craft store. But, I'll take it.

I doubt Dad would have guessed his worn boots would be the object of decades-old sentiment, but there they sit, on my table. I'm nine years old again, ready for the chance to be by my Dad's side. So, in a way, he is still by mine. ✻

On The Square

Dear Dad,

You would get a kick out of downtown Ocala these days. Your beloved "Courthouse Square" has become a thriving hub of activity. I mean, this place is alive! Just yesterday, I drove around the square for 15 minutes in search of a place to park because the parking garage was full.

Yes, a parking garage. We have one now. Condominiums and lofts, too! Who'd of thunk?

Well, you did, actually. You often told me how downtown was our county's best kept secret. As a builder in charge of a few construction projects just off the square, you had a vision for a multi-use community plan although you didn't call it that. Such labels would have seemed too "high falootin" for your sensibilities. But, oh how things have come together, Dad.

You'd be pleased to know your youngest daughter has your downtown-love DNA. So do a lot of others. Our city leaders and volunteers have fostered an environment of growth and creativity on every block. Remember the Woolworth building, Riley's Grocery Store and the Dixie Theatre? They've been transformed into diverse businesses. Just try to get a table on a Saturday night at any restaurant without waiting.

And the Marion Theatre shows first-run films and serves the best popcorn and wine. No more prohibition here!

It's a no brainer when Mike and I have a free night. We head downtown, enjoy our choice of a fine meal on any corner, catch a movie at the Marion Theatre, then walk around and see the downtown sites. Often, a free concert is taking place on the square or at City Hall's Citizens' Circle. And the old City Auditorium at Tuscawilla Park is now the Reilly Arts Center, a first-class performing arts center that hosts our own orchestra.

Yep, we have an orchestra, Dad. And it's surrounded by art, science and inspiration.

Are you ready for this? We have a local farmers market next to City Hall with food trucks, a modern version of the ice cream truck that would come by our house when school let out, only these trucks sell burritos and café con leche.

Dad, I miss you every day, but especially so when I find myself anywhere close to Main and Magnolia. I go to your downtown homage, your book "The Courthouse Square" and open a cornered page that reminds me why I love this place so much. You wrote:

"Prosperity was just around the corner. What corner? The heart and soul of man would not be defeated. Walking the Square on a Saturday afternoon were people who were not well off, but held onto an indestructible belief that things had to get better. The enigma of it all. That when life was hard and harsh, there was still tenderness and compassion. Through it all there was a time of innocence, fellowship, conviction and optimism. And we felt it on the Square."

I'd like to think such fellowship is alive and well on your beloved Square. We still feel it.

In fact, some of Ocala's best marketing minds developed a "Feel Downtown Ocala" branding initiative, touting all our city has to offer. Walking on the Square this past Saturday were people who came to be a part of something special, be it a shared meal, concert, or sense of community. I was there, too.

And so were you, Dad.

All my love,

Your Downtown-Loving Daughter ❧

Right Where I Belong

*I*f your life has turned out exactly the way you planned, this column is not for you.

If, however, you've had a front row seat to life's curveballs, some good, some not so, keep reading. You are among a kindred spirit. And by kindred spirit, I mean a middle-aged woman sitting in a coffee shop in her hometown, the place she once swore she'd never, never return to after high school. Should've skipped that extra "never." I once had a flair for hyperbole.

I also once said I'd travel the four corners of the world because I was 8 years old and I'd heard someone say that. Plus, I thought there were, literally, four corners from one end of the earth to the other. Thank goodness for geography class.

Next to global travel, I kept other dreams in a lime green leather diary with a lock and key cleverly titled as "Amy's Dreams." Then I lost the key. Then the journal. But, the dreams were still there, deep in the heart of an impressionable young girl who thought proclaiming to leave home for good was the only way to fulfillment.

Some of my dreams were, and still are, worth pursuing. But a lot of them were really a delusional form of desire masked as a fantasy, usually someone else's fantasy because it sounded exciting and so utterly different from the life I was living. Different was what I was shooting for.

One thing I never scribbled in my journal was the notion of contentment. Who wants that? To me, contentment inferred settling, and settling meant living smack in the middle of unfulfilled plans and hopes in a town far too small for someone with big honkin' dreams.

Then I grew up. And I left home. And I came back. And I left again. Came back. Well, you know the drill.

Along the way, I made a few dreams come true while also racking up a few big honkin' failures. Homer Simpson said, "Trying is the first step toward failure." Boy, did I try spectacularly. And you know what? I wouldn't change a thing.

Seriously?

Of course I would! I'd change a lime green diary full of choices I made or choices I had to make that were out of my control — i.e. most of what life is made of.

But, gracious, life is also made of beautiful unrealized dreams, too, some that take you right back to where you never, never thought you'd be. Like back home.

Down the road from the coffee shop is a local French restaurant where Mike and I can be found most Friday nights. We have our spot at the end of the bar where Pablo makes our favorite cocktails. The owners and I catch up on each other's families as local musicians perform as good as anywhere I've been. Friends stop by for a few hellos on their way to their seats, and strangers sit next to us. By the time we leave, they usually become new friends.

This is our place, I say to Mike.

The last scene in "Something's Gotta Give" has Jack Nicholson beaming as he sits at a table in a restaurant with his wife and new grandbaby. He's beaming from ear to ear, like look at me, I've found it — everything I wanted.

And what did he want? Riches? Fame? Fortune? No, spoiler alert: He had those earlier in the film and things didn't go so well. He found joy, love, contentment. In a place he never thought he'd be.

That's how I feel in the place I never thought I'd be. Wherever I am, at my favorite French place or home or the bookstore, I sometimes glance around, beaming.

I've found it.

Joseph Campbell said, "We must let go of the life we had planned, so as to accept the one that is waiting for us. Usually, mine is waiting for me on the corner of Fort King Street and First Avenue. ❄

Our Porch

My dad never met a front porch he didn't like. Curious, then, that he never had one in the Ocala homes he built as a residential contractor. His front entrances usually consisted of a few concrete steps leading up to an entry barely big enough to hold a plant, let alone a rocking chair. Yet, he often waxed poetically about what he called "front porch living."

"Porches were an extension of the living room. During the long, hot summer days and nights, families moved out to the porches, especially at night. After supper was over and the dishes washed, you sat on the front porch and talked," Dad wrote in this very newspaper many years ago.

In addition to being a darn good builder, Dad was also a writer. He penned a few self-published books about living in Ocala, serving our country and the Allied forces in World War II, as well as about falling in love with a local girl he met in his teens while swinging on her dad's front porch swing.

"Young folks would dream dreams, swing miles and miles. Most of their courting would be done on the front porch swing," Dad wrote. "Nelwyn's father was a deacon in the Baptist church. After church on Sunday night, they would usually have called a deacon's meeting. We ran home so we could have a few moments alone on the front porch swing."

Mama turns 94 this week. She's been without Dad for a long time. I keep one of his books in my purse to read to her when I visit her at the nursing home. I select a few passages from my favorites of the first of his multiple book collection, "The Story Pole."

Dad would totally get a kick of thinking he had a literary collection. He wrote this book in his mid-50s when work and life slowed down enough for him to pound out thoughts on his typewriter in his home office next to a pile of architectural sketches of building projects. A friend copyedited, and another friend printed a few hundred copies. He sold out within a week. Later, he printed a few more copies at a local office supply store, some with the pages upside down. I possess a few of these versions and love them for their publishing imperfection.

Sometimes, the words I read to Mama don't resonate; other times, they do. Without fail, her connection is always when it's about her relationship with Dad. When I ask her about courting on the porch, she smiles, but says nothing. Maybe that's how it should be, time locked just between the two of them.

Nothing reminds you of fleeting days and nights than caring for an elderly parent. I am my father's age when he penned the story I now read to his widow.

"The days of rocking chairs, swings, front porches, the good times, the bad times and the quiet ties have come to pass and gone on," Dad remembered. "This way of life will never be the same. We who were there will smile and remember when the whippoorwill sang."

Dad may have never had a front porch, but he perfectly captured the essence of what it meant to have a sacred place to commune and dream.

For this, I wish my mother the happiest of days. And to my father, I remain forever grateful for the reminder of finding solace at home, be it a front porch or the memory of one. ❊

My Own Stars Hollow

My daughter often says Ocala is a lot like Stars Hollow, the quaint and intimate town in the TV show "Gilmore Girls." I recently had an experience that confirms her observation, and it began and ended with buying orthopedic shoes.

Back story: for the past few months, I've struggled with chronic foot issues resulting in throbbing heel and arch pain. The fact that I was even talking about heel and arch pain made me want to hide under my bed covers and wake up to be 20 again when life was fresh and bold with three-inch heels. Not an option, my doctor said after he examined the source of my pain. He informed me this is often a natural part of aging and too much foot stress inflames an already vulnerable situation. I joked this was probably the result of running too many marathons, but he wasn't buying it. "Get supportive shoes," he said as his nurse handed me a shoe buying guide.

Twenty minutes later, I was limping into a department store with one goal: buy the most chic kind of ortho shoes I could find. I quickly passed by my old friends — Michael Kors, Ralph Lauren, Sam Edelman — all had been good to me for many years with their stylish shoes that made me feel glamorous. Now their shoes made me feel like I was ankle-deep in a bucket of nails. So long, Mike, Ralph and Sam, arch support is what I'm after!

I was on my sixteenth pair of shoes when I noticed two women were staring at me.

"Oh, that's not a good look," one said, shaking her head as she eyed my selections. "You can do better."

Before I could protest and ask who the heck she thought she was, her friend handed me two more pairs of shoes off the rack.

"Try these," she said. "They look great, and you can walk in them longer than five minutes."

They were right. Slipping on the low-heel shoe, I thought I heard angels singing as my aching foot rested on a pillow of leather. Skipping down the shoe aisle, I high-fived my new friends as they cheered me right past the ortho sneakers. When I turned around, more women had gathered nodding their heads in approval.

Soon, I was swiping my debit card for three pairs of shoes I could wear for "work and play" according to Barbara, my new shoe BFF. After a parting goodbye, I wore one of my new purchases right out of the box and wandered into the women's casual wear department feeling young, bold and confident.

"Hey!" someone yelled. "Look at this!"

My shoe buddies held up a dress. "This would go great with your gold shoes!"

Right again. We all laughed how the shoe stars had aligned for me, but, really, I was lucky to run into a group of women who decided their temporary mission in life was to get me on the ortho fashion track for success.

These were my people now. They invited me to go for an after-work drink. But I begged off, so we exchanged contact info.

"Amy Mangan?" one of them said, "Are you Sherman Yeary's daughter?"

And just like that, we discovered a connection through a friend of my father's.

"Wait a minute, I know your mom," another shoe pal said.

This would totally have happened in "Gilmore Girls," only over a cup of coffee at Luke's Diner. Almost like Stars Hollow, only better, right here in the town that gave me new arch and friend support. And yet another reason I love Ocala so. ❁

The Breakfast Club

*T*here's a familiar ache when I drive past Wolfy's Restaurant, the place where my father met for breakfast for almost two decades with a group of friends they called the Breakfast Club. Seldom did any of them miss their weekly gathering. They were the boys of Ocala High School, class of 1940, give or take a year between them. They became the soldiers of World War II, then husbands, fathers, grandfathers, and, for some, widows. Only three members of the club—who once boasted of 20 men – haven't succumbed to old age, illness or tragedy.

The back corner of the restaurant was reserved for them with tables pushed together to accommodate everyone. Still, it was tight, so latecomers would squeeze in elbow to elbow, and steal an extra fork from their buddy.

I had the privilege to be their guest for breakfast once—an honor bestowed only to a lucky few. I think my invitation was secured not because I was Sherman's daughter, although that probably had something to do with it, but because I was writing a local feature about them. They were in rare form, cutting up and joking with one another for the sake of their visiting scribe. They shared stories of high school pranks, football victories, and life in a small town. Breakfast ended by settling up on the weekly bet—usually about a sports event of some kind. The winner got breakfast paid for and a little extra spending money.

As the years progressed, the club became diligent about their weekly time together. If one member was feeling poorly, someone else would pick him up for breakfast so he wouldn't have to drive. Only vacations and hospital stays precluded attendance and spouses knew better than to plan something on a Wednesday morning.

And they were there, too, at the funeral of my father who left implicit instructions that when he died, he wanted a special section at the church reserved for the Breakfast Club. They sat together, elbow to fragile elbow, in suits that hung on their wrinkled frames.

I think of my hastily scheduled and infrequent lunches with girlfriends. A quick cell phone call usually confirms lunch. First one who gets to the restaurant orders sweet tea for everyone. Try to get a booth. Four of us will be there. And so we rush in, frantic from the day's assortment of meetings, school programs, and budding crises. By mid-lunch, we begin to subtly check our watches because we have to be somewhere else in half and hour. We always have to be somewhere else in half an hour. So the conversation is clipped, though not economical in spirit. In spite of the mental distractions, we get a lot in. Talk of children, spouses, work, politics, hopes, fears, and the grocery list are sprinkled in between passing the mustard for our sandwiches.

Many of these friendships have now spanned decades, too, just like dad's club coterie. We've gone through college, husbands, babies, jobs, and mortgages. I'm not as good as Dad in reserving a regular spot on the calendar for friends, but I'd like to be.

I wonder what my lunch group will say to one another 20 years from now? The context will change though I suspect the dialogue will be even richer and deeper. Talk of retirement, grandkids, mountain homes, and dreams will layer our time together...if we're lucky. This much I know I'd like to say to them as we sit, elbow to elbow, in a crowded booth—"Thank you." ❄

HEART

A Marriage for the Movies

I got married this past weekend. It was a last-minute decision after driving home from dinner downtown. The only guests were our children, who were in the car with Mike and me. We pulled over to a vacant lot for our ad hoc ceremony. Mike didn't turn off the car; instead, he switched on his hazard lights and left the driver's door open (maybe for a quick pre-wedding jitters escape?). It may have been the shortest wedding ever, except for one technicality: we were already married.

Which is why we decided to do it all over again.

This month marks our 25th year of marriage, a milestone that reassures and confounds me. There is beauty in longevity and shared history and I'm a big fan of both. I have always liked the knowing part of life. Confession: I sometimes read a movie spoiler before seeing a film. If you saw "Interstellar," you'd understand. Being married is like a movie – full of drama, romance, comedy and an occasional cliffhanger. Except there are no spoilers revealing what will happen in advance.

In marriage there is also beauty in what you don't know. If, many years ago, I'd have seen the Mangan Marriage Spoiler Trailer of challenges Mike and I would face, I would have put down my large bag of buttered popcorn, sprinted back to the ticket booth and demanded a showing of the Norah Ephron version of us. Not the one Francis Ford Coppola would have directed all dark and ominous with sad violin music playing in the background. Give me light and happy. With an upbeat soundtrack. And Tom Hanks and Meg Ryan.

But that's not the real world or a real marriage. And here is the part that confounds me still after 25 years – the real parts of being together have become the very heart of what makes us, well, us. When we've been scared and worried and stressed. When reality hits us square in the eyes.

We find a way. Goodness knows, I'm thankful for the happy times. Yet, when the weight of our world is sitting on top of my chest, I find comfort in knowing that Mike is beside me to lighten the load.

We've had our share of hard. But we wake up every day doing what we have done from day one in our marriage. We find a way to get through the difficult and inhale the easy when it comes along. And we never, ever forget all that we have: two amazing children with a network of family and friends in a community of love like nothing I've ever seen anywhere else.

And we have each other.

For the past three months, our family has been in a required hibernation. We've either been at home or in a hospital. So dinner downtown was a rare treat, a perfect time for an anniversary celebration. On the drive home, Mike turned down a street to show the children the church where we were married.

A fire claimed First Baptist Church decades ago. All that is left is the vacant property. It took about a second for us to decide a wedding was in order. We hopped out of the car laughing like school kids. Griffin walked me down the grassy aisle as Gilly and Mike waited in the middle of the lot. Holding hands, Mike and I shared what it meant to be married to each other. As we kissed, I looked up and saw a shooting star in the chilly, star-lit sky. But it was actually an airplane.

Just like a Norah Ephron movie. Almost. ❄

Loss, Love and a Ukelele

Perspective comes in the most surprising places. Like the doctor's waiting room that held me hostage for two hours past my appointment. The first hour wasn't so bad. I thumbed through magazines and caught up on Katy Perry's feud with Taylor Swift. Then I scanned emails on my phone while trying to ignore the television's programmed medical show about preventative care for certain anatomical organs.

By the second hour, I was growing irritated. I had work to do, calls to make, errands to run. A few people were called into the inner sanctum to see the doctor, but none came back out, like the first season of "Stranger Things."

My fellow patients were losing their patience, too.

"I guess this is why they call it 'a waiting room,'" said an older man sitting next to me.

Everyone nodded, unified in our discontent. Others chimed in, sharing how long they had been waiting. One woman suggested we approach en masse the reception office assistant and demand answers. Vive la revolution!

Just as I was ready to storm the office fortress, I glanced at my cell phone. A text from a friend said she had sad news. A mutual friend's husband had died unexpectedly. Then I received a social media alert that one of my favorite writers lost her 57-year-old partner to cancer.

I looked up. Most of my waiting room revolutionaries were older and alone.

Across the room was a frail, silver-haired woman staring out the window. I hadn't noticed her earlier. She and her late husband had owned a local business that is now run by her son. For over 50 years, she scheduled appointments while her husband managed the rest. They did everything together. Often, I'd see them at lunch sitting shoulder-to-shoulder on the same side of the booth at the pizza place across the street from their shop.

The man sitting on my left told me he'd lost his wife last summer. Evenings are the hardest, he said. His children and grandchildren live up north. They want him to move closer, but this is home he said to me before quickly looking away, mindful that maybe he said too much to a stranger.

Then I looked at the man to my right. Dignified with handsome features and a thick head of wavy gray hair, he was wearing a nicely pressed button-down shirt tucked into jeans. This man I know well. He is my husband. We don't normally go to doctors' appointments together, but I was having a minor procedure that required someone to drive me home. As the hours went by, I encouraged Mike to leave. I'd call him when I was ready. No sense in both of us stuck in the waiting room with a TV medical show — the background music consisting of a ukulele and cymbal.

"Nope, I'm staying," he said, squeezing my hand. "Maybe we can get everybody to join in singing to the ukulele."

Mike added his own song verse that rhymed with those certain anatomical organs featured on the TV. We started laughing, unable to stop, then crying, punchy from our marathon in a doctor's office with a cheery healthcare musical.

Finally regaining a semblance of composure, I took a deep breath. I placed my cell phone in my purse and focused on my husband, the comic. We talked about our schedule for the rest of the day, what to make for dinner that night, plans for the weekend. Nothing serious, but it sure beat reading about the Kardashians and fretting over missing time from work, calls, and errands.

I'm pretty sure the man sitting to my left and the frail, silver-haired woman across the room and my friend who just lost her husband would give anything for a few more minutes of everyday conversation with their loved ones. One day, one of us won't be here — Mike and me — leaving the other to wait alone for appointments.

Shoulder-to-shoulder we sat beside each other and talked and waited. When the nurse called my name, I looked at Mike.

"I'll be right here," he said.

Four words that we can never take for granted. ❄

The Movie Club

atching the Academy Awards made me cry though not because "Mad Max: Fury Road" swept the Oscars.

I got misty because I missed my friends. A long time ago in a galaxy far, far away existed a magical group known as The Movie Club. Three couples came together because we discovered our mutual obsession with fine cinema, although fine and cinema could be debated (we once watched "Bringing Down the House" with Steve Martin and Queen Latifah because it was slim pickings at the theater).

What began as an occasional social outing evolved into a monthly movie night for more than 15 years with a group of acquaintances who became some of the truest friends I've ever had. And then they moved.

If The Movie Club were a screenplay, it would include compelling storylines for sure. We had rich character development — each of us grew through the course of our time together. Our lives shaped and reshaped us into who we aspired to be and, sometimes, who we needed to be: engaged community leaders, effective managers, diligent and protective caregivers, crisis counselors. We changed jobs, hobbies and houses, especially the latter. Collectively, we moved 12 times, I think. At one point, we all lived on the same street, which turned our movie club into a spontaneous wine club, walking to each other's homes for an early evening glass of Pinot.

There was a strong narrative arc to our group, too. We shared the loss of loved ones together. Some of the children got married and had children. Two of the husbands had heart catheterizations. The recession hit a few of us hard.

We faced disappointment, heartache and transitions together, all the more the reason to celebrate happiness. We took birthdays to a whole new celebratory level. Fitting for a movie club, we embraced the concept of a

theme. We surprised Sara, our politically-savvy club member, with a red, white and blue dinner. Hellen got a gourmet cooking class and Walt, the pilot, an aviation-themed night. We once held a surprise "anti-party" for Chick, always the humble one who tried to avoid the birthday spotlight. Not a chance, mister. Our entire dinner centered around a faux celebration of everyone and everything but him. We toasted the neighbor down the street and the wine glasses on the table. Of course, we got around to honoring the birthday boy.

Oh, and we watched movies.

Lots of them.

Our usual routine included catching a late-afternoon matinee with dinner after to offer our film critiques. It's remarkable to think of it now, given all the things we had going on in our lives, but we seldom missed a month together at the theater. Sometimes, if nothing good was on, we'd end up at one of our homes and watch a rental. We kept a list of the movies we'd seen, though none of us could agree on the first movie we first saw together.

And you can't have a movie club without honoring the big cinematic kahuna of them all, the annual Academy Awards. We went all out with our Oscar parties – the food represented the nominated films. English Tea Cakes for "Gosford Park," French for "Something's Gotta Give." But, like any good film, our story came to an end. Walt and Hellen moved out of town first, then Chick and Sara. Mike and I are still here. Each year we turn on the TV and watch about half an hour of the Oscars, but it's not the same.

Cue the closing credits. And the memories of a movie club that once was and always will be Oscar worthy in friendship to me.

The 2 a.m. Call

ho can you call at 2 a.m.?

This question was posed by a friend at dinner with my husband and me. We were talking about life and all its crazy twists and turns and, in particular, our friendship. While we seldom see each other — our dinner was rare and welcome — it was surprisingly lovely to hear him say that Mike and I are on his "2 a.m. call list" if he had an emergency. This got me thinking: Who can I call at 2 a.m.?

Sure, I am fortunate to have a wide net of acquaintances. Yet who is really with me when the going gets rough and takes the whole thick-or-thin notion to a higher level?

I conducted a mental inventory of what qualifies to meet such a distinction. Here is what I realized:

Two a.m. friends will:

- *Say "I'll be right there" after you call with an urgent request.*
- *Lament at your injustices, real or perceived, and wisely wait to tell you otherwise after the emotional intensity has been turned down a notch.*
- *Show up at your doorstep with (a) a pan of lasagna (b) brownies (c) Betty Cakes (d) all of the above.*
- *Listen from the heart.*
- *Not try to fix your problem. He/she knows better.*
- *Tell you when to slow down.*
- *Tell you when to get moving past whatever inertia is bogging you down.*
- *Gently suggest you should put down that third serving of Betty Cakes. Too much of a good thing is, well, you know ...*

Conversely, 2 a.m. friends will not:
- *Immediately say you are wrong about an issue.*
- *Give advice unless you've asked for it.*
- *Ask questions when you need presence and nothing else.*
- *Ignore your call, email, text.*
- *Hold his/her own grudge over a slight or argument you've both forgotten what its origin was to begin with.*
- *Crush from the weight of what you're dealing with.*

Goodness knows I'm an expert on emergency calls, none by design. And it's not just 2 a.m. — that's a metaphor, right? — it's anytime. When you need help and can't even articulate what kind of help you need. You just need it. Period.

In my life and relationships, I ascribe to a motto that I stole from my daughter's place of employment. She works for a critical care teen/life program at a teaching hospital. Its mission statement includes this simple, yet beautiful, principle: "We carry each other."

A 2 a.m. friend carries you when you are too tired to walk or form a complete sentence or think about the next hour, let alone the next day or year.

A 2 a.m. friend carries you through another person's betrayals, your own failures (and you'll have plenty) and your own successes (you'll have plenty, but be careful, those are often paved with more landmines than your failures). You name it, you're carried, in big ways and small.

I don't know what tomorrow holds. Or tonight for that matter. What I do know is I've got emotional insurance by those who will answer my call if I need them, 2 a.m. or otherwise.

And what if they need me?

Rest assured, I'll answer. No matter what. We carry each other. ❈

For Certain

For once, I had written this column in advance, a rarity for a procrastinator like me. Hurricane Irma inspired me to craft my thoughts around a post-storm life and expectations. I was ready to hit my computer's "send" button when I heard that a 50-year-old woman I knew had unexpectedly died.

Suddenly, meandering on about a privileged society dependent on first-world luxuries like reliable electricity rang hollow. All that I was left with was a blank page and broken heart.

I stepped away from the laptop unsure how to frame a sentence, let alone an essay. That's when my friend called me. This loss cut deep for her. And for the next few minutes, we cried together for a life that no longer was, for a husband and young daughter whose wife and mother was gone, for the brutal randomness of it all.

After a couple of minutes, I asked how I could help. My friend paused, still trying to collect herself, then took a deep breath and began her response with, "OK, here's what I think the family will need ..."

She kicked into emotional warrior mode, part wobbly, part fierce, wholly determined to do something. Within the next 24 hours, my friend and many others rallied to do a lot of things — arrange for daily meal deliveries for the family, send memorial donations to the daughter's school, and so much more, most of which I don't even know about.

But what I did witness was a universal offering of unconditional love.

Such kindness isn't limited to my beloved hometown. Our world is filled with wobbly/fierce/determined emotional warriors who show up and shower love to the wounded. And just as we step in to help, I've noticed that we also go through our own kind of grief, distant or far to the unimaginable pain that becomes soul-crushingly real.

As I scanned my original column, there was one applicable part worth salvaging:

Life is a privilege like that of dependable electricity. There is nothing we can do to prevent a storm from ravaging our lives or that of those whom we love. We will be plunged into the darkness, lost and empty among the debris and chaos of a life without order. We will seek refuge. We will be comforted. And when a storm impacts someone else, we will be their refuge. That's how it goes.

However, this past week, I've been mulling this privilege concept. You see, I kind of forgot this thing called life is a privilege, not a right. Me, of all people, the overtly compassionate mom/wife/daughter/sister who ends practically every conversation, call, visit or text with "I love you" to those whom I can't imagine a life without.

"I'm going to do a load of laundry. I love you."

"Good luck on your test! I love you."

"Do you want to grab lunch? I love you."

Yet, in between all these love shout-outs, the rest of my life has gotten assumed. And by this I mean I assume there will be a tomorrow. I assume I'll have a chance to baste another turkey, decorate another Christmas tree, share another "I love you" on the way to filling up my car with gas.

I definitely score in the upper atta-girl quadrant of telling others how I feel, but I'm deficient in the actual doing part. I beg off time with friends because there is something else I have to do. I dream about sharing fun experiences with my family, but days turn into months without chalking up adventures worth remembering. I say "no" more than I say "yes" to fully living each day.

If there is any comfort while mourning this most recent loss of life, here is one thing I know: Just this past year, she, too, re-evaluated the priorities in her life and made a change that gave her more time with and attention to those she loved. No regrets there. No assumptions. She made the most of her time here.

So, in her honor, I'm working hard to make the most of each day — heck, hour. No matter how hard you prepare, storms will come. It's not about how prepared you are, but, rather, how present you were before they arrived. ✺

Our Story

Everyone's suicide story is both unique and similar. Mine is no different. My brother-in-law ended his life and, as such, moved my family from the known to the unknowable. In an instant, my sister, her young children, my parents, my other sisters and I were catapulted into a life not of our choosing. I don't profess to know the half of it. I was 17 years old when it happened. We all did our best to fill in the cracks, yet, 36 years later, we still trip into emotional quicksand.

You have a story, I bet. So does your neighbor. Your co-worker. Your best friend. Someone you knew of who found the weight of the world too heavy and made a choice that seemed like the only option.

I should tell you this is not a column about suicide prevention. Rather — and hear me out — I'd like to explore the notion of acceptance. Goodness knows, I'd give anything to have my brother-in-law back. And others who've left. My grad school friend. My dear girlfriend's husband. Robin Williams. Anthony Bourdain. Kate Spade.

Through the years, I saw the toll our loss took on my family. The birthdays, anniversaries and graduations that never were. He wasn't there.

For many years, we fell into the "I wishes." I wish we'd have done better in finding professional help in the shadow of the stigma — a Vietnam veteran with post-traumatic stress. Resources and receptiveness for his condition were limited. I wish we could've told him more emphatically how loved he was, how his creative energy inspired us all. He had a vineyard in Ocala just for the fun of it. Who does that? He did. And he played the banjo with a smile that melted you.

I wish he knew that. Maybe he did? Thus, we fell down an endless rabbit hole.

Acceptance was harder to swallow. It happened. But his absence haunted us for years. Acceptance of what happened would never bring him back. But it might just have saved a part of us that we lost in the maelstrom of trying to figure out what could have been done to prevent it. As I write this, I find myself hesitant to go deeper, afraid to reopen the wound out of sensitivity to those closer to the eternal fire. Grief has no shelf life.

So much is written about lessons of life. Here's the lesson I learned: Sometimes you look so hard for meaning, for a reason why, that you miss the who. Who is left in the shadow of the coda? Who could use someone to just show up? Again. And again, long after the loss. Long after others return to their corner of life that, for many, seems infinitely rich and normal and forever unattainable.

The day before my brother-in-law's funeral, a friend brought my sister a gift of the most beautiful silk blouse. It fit her perfectly, framing her shoulders rounded by circumstance and pain. Yet there are moments since that my sister wears this blouse, almost 40 years later, and, to me, is at her most whole. A piece of clothing chosen with intention and care.

Writer Anna Quindlen said of her mother's early death that when someone asks when the hurt stops, she always replies, "If it ever does, I will let you know."

And until it does, let's give what we can to those who are hurting — love. ❀

The Sweetest Name

I'm trying to make sense of something that doesn't make sense. Throughout my life, I've experienced loss. I've seen loved ones leave this world after long struggles with serious illnesses. I've watched tragedies unfold of friends gone too soon. Yet, for many of these losses, there's been a natural course of things. However, I recently said goodbye to someone who should still be here—my nephew, Josh Moody, who died suddenly at the age of 29.

So I can only find the words to acknowledge what I know rather than what I don't understand. Josh had his life in front of him. He had evolved from an adolescent young man named Joshua who had an affinity for odd and curious pets like snakes that his patient mother would let him keep. He grew into an articulate young businessman called Josh who fulfilled his dream by returning to the place that meant so much to him—Jacksonville Beach.

I know his return to the ocean was as much metaphorical as practical. He had established his own medical supply company there. He had just recently purchased his first home, a hip two-bedroom condo just a block and a half away from the ocean. That's when he became the Moodz—his surfing name given to him by his cadre of surfing buddies and college fraternity friends.

In time, our family began calling him Joshie because this seemed to help us transition him from the world we knew of Joshua to the professional world in which Josh began living. And it was a good life.

He formed his own business. He created an extensive and diverse network of professional and personal friends that many of us only

dream about. He found his passion in medical sales and ocean surfing—somewhere in this I'm certain there's an apt parallel.

There's one title he never shied away, bestowed upon him at birth—Joshua Yeary Moody—his middle name given to him in honor of his mother's—my sister's—maiden name. You see, there were four Yeary girls, which made it rather evident the line of succession would not endure unless one of us peaked with a burst of liberation. His parents gave him his middle name as a symbol of connecting generations, past and present. Josh knew this and wore it well, always bridging relationships between both families. In many ways, he was our generational glue.

At an early age, Josh had to assume a new and different title—that of father to his younger sister Molly and caregiver to his mother Julie. His father died—also too soon—when Josh and Molly were very young.

And when Joshua Yeary Moody died, he was buried next to his father. He assumed a position he'd wanted all of his life—that of father and son together.

Joshua. Josh. Moodz. Joshie. Friend, businessman, son, nephew, brother, grandson, boyfriend, surrogate father, and family protector. Joshua Yeary Moody, it was never about who you were—it was always about who you had become. Thank you for showing me that names really do mean something.

I will always love you, sweet Joshie. �֍

Compassion at a Crowded Gate

I was almost at the Orlando International Airport entrance when a Transportation Security Administration officer fell to his death. After the officer jumped from the airport's inside hotel balcony into the atrium area, confused travelers ran past security causing grounded flights. My daughter, flying in from Birmingham, called to say all flights into Orlando were indefinitely delayed. For a minute, I considered turning around my car to return home. Instead, I headed to the airport.

I'm glad I did.

For the next five hours, I was reminded of what I love most about humanity — the people. While this sentiment sounds like a Yogi Berra misquote, it's true. Shortly after the initial chaos of the tragedy subsided, fear turned into mercy.

When the parking lot escalator took me into the main terminal, massive lines snaked through the airport unlike anything I'd ever seen. Thousands of stranded travelers were huddled together without view of security checkpoints. Overtired children clung to their parents. Families split up — some sat on the floor by the walls, while others stayed in line so as not to lose their place. The arrival and departures screens lit up like a Christmas tree with one word "DELAY."

"It's best I not look at it," a young mom with 5-year-old twin daughters said pointing to the departures screen. She was flying home to New York after a week at Walt Disney World, evident by the pink glitter Mickey Mouse ears adorned on her girls who started to cry when they couldn't find a place to sit to eat their late lunch. "They are past the point of reasoning," she said with a weary half-smile any parent could relate to.

That's when an older man offered his chair. Then another couple quickly cleaned up their adjoining table and offered their seats as they asked the girls about their favorite part about Disney. Later, out of earshot from the mother and her girls, they told me they stood in line for three hours before finding out their flight had been cancelled.

Sitting on a bench near the arrival gate, I watched so many acts of kindness I stopped counting. The elderly woman who gave up her spot in line to a college student who was trying to make a connecting flight. The couple from Apopka who offered their home to anyone who needed a place to spend the night.

My husband, a Florida native and multiple hurricane survivor, often says we see the best in most people during a crisis. I had a front row seat to such goodness at the airport. Amidst the angst of what had happened, of the sadness, the uncertainty, there was an unspoken reverence and grace.

To quote writer Glennon Doyle Melton, it was "brutiful," equal parts brutal and beautiful.

Gilly texted to say her flight would arrive after all, as day turned into dusk. Standing at the entry of the arrival gate, I saw a TSA officer. I thanked him for his service, acknowledging his loss. He paused, then thanked me; he had known his lost colleague.

"This is the hardest day of my life," he said. "And I was here on 9/11."

This reminded me of another part of humanity, the kind that leads to hubris, to declarations of decisions that make great soundbites but result in horrific outcomes. Words and actions matter. As do paychecks. Just ask federal workers, like TSA officers, required to work for 35 days without pay. I don't know if the fallen officer was a part of the mandated furlough to work without pay, but I do know he felt the burden, evident by what he shared with coworkers before his suicide.

It's easy to see why Americans poll at an all-time low for their faith in government. They expect better. The airport tragedy could easily be, and probably will be, politicized. This is a mistake. It's not about liberals or conservatives. None of this was present as I stood in the concourse. Instead, I witnessed discreet miracles of compassion for tired and lost strangers.

Maybe this is where we begin to rebuild a sense of unity in our country. We are all fellow travelers trying to get home. ❋

So Long, Honey

'm not the first person to lose a dog. Nor is this the first dog I've lost. Yet, I find myself free falling in an alternate universe of grief unlike anything I've experienced.

This one hurts deeply, not only because I've lost "the sweetest puppy in the whole wide world" — a subtitle we bequeathed to our four-pound puddle of white fur when we got her — but also because my husband, children and I were loved so purely by her furry sweetness for many years. Honey would have been 14 on Friday, an occasion that would call for a birthday hat, Twistee Treat pup cup and presents. Lots of presents.

But, two weeks earlier, Honey's heart gave out quickly and unexpectedly, maybe because she gave so much of it to us her entire life.

I believe there are two kinds of dog owners: those who have dogs as pets and those who have dogs as family. We fell into the latter.

We started out as pet owners the first day we brought Honey, a tiny Chihuahua Poodle mix, home with every intention to keep her in the oversized kennel in the laundry room. That lasted until midnight when Mike "rescued" (his words, not mine) our crying Chi-Poo from her "prison" (again, his words) and plopped square in the middle of our bed, a spot she kept for the rest of her life. She became family that night and, as such, I offer this obituary in her honor.

Honey Bun "H.B." Mangan,
The Sweetest Puppy in the Whole Wide World

Ocala — Honey Mangan passed away on Sept. 21, 2016. A longtime resident of Ocala, Honey was born on Oct. 14, 2002, in Belleview,

Florida before being rescued by a family of four, whom she rescued with love in return.

She was a graduate of Pet Smart's Puppy Training, but just barely. She repeatedly failed the impulse-control exercises, looking at her owners as if to say, "Is this really necessary?" She was a compassionate caregiver to her human dad, mom, brother and sister — encouraging them to join her in her affinity for long naps, soft blankets and a really good piece of cheddar cheese.

She became an avid photo hound, literally. She loved the camera and vice versa. Honey was the original photo bomber. Holidays were her favorite mainly because it was an opportunity to open presents. On Christmas morning, she would sit on the couch waiting her turn to open her gifts, excitedly ripping the paper with her teeth in gleeful abandon. Then she'd hop off the couch and stand by her stocking filled with treats and toys until someone with good sense would take the darn sock off the mantle.

Sometimes, Honey was the source of inspiration for her mom's writing, so often attracting the most reader feedback that mom considered being a one-topic/one-dog writer.

Honey is survived by her loving dad, Mike; mom, Amy; and two siblings, Griffin and Gillian. She eased their pain when life got rough, instinctively knowing when someone needed extra attention. A celebration of her life was attempted last weekend when the children came home from college, but the emptiness in the house where Honey lived and ruled was too present. So, the family has decided that every day will be a celebration of life because Honey remains in the everyday moments.

In lieu of flowers, Honey's family would like you to honor her memory by doing exactly what she did for almost 14 years of her life: love others freely. And take long naps with a soft blanket from time to time. ❋

MAMA MANGZ

The Mom Box

Growing up in Ocala I was lucky to be surrounded by my hometown's own version of Steel Magnolias: strong, fearless women who could host a dinner party, balance work, and life, and manage a crisis all at the same time. Grit and grace were part of their DNA.

Two of them passed away last week. Once again, I'm reminded how death instructs the living.

Eulogies and Facebook tributes aside, I tend to drill down on a personal level to define what made the loss so uniquely hard. They both died suddenly. They were intensely beloved by their families and community and were genuinely good, like an angelic selfless kind of good. Their deaths elicited a universal emotional response – oh no, not her.

Often in life, we put people in boxes with clearly defined roles. At first, Pat Ball and Brenda Adolf were in the mom box to me. I grew up with their children. I vacationed with one (Pat) and spent many a night at the other's home (Brenda). They both wrapped me under their maternal wings, which had to be a comfort to my mom, who had already raised three daughters and was in her 40s raising little ole full-of-life me.

As I got older, my relationship with Pat and Brenda evolved into the friendship box, even though this doesn't seem to quite fit the bill for what they meant to me.

I don't remember when I didn't know Miss Pat. She was always in my life. She and her husband, Tommy, were among my parents' best friends.

They went to church together, raised children, played Rummy on the weekends, and stayed at the Daytona Beach hotel every summer. Our families were part of a circle of friends in Ocala that was so tight, so entwined in one another's lives, that I often felt like I had multiple sets of parents. And the Balls took this role seriously. So much, in fact, they almost killed me.

Pat and Tommy were my church youth group leaders. They taught us scripture during Sunday school, took us on lake retreats and introduced us to their fondness for fitness. The latter is what got me.

One Saturday, the Balls thought it would be fun to take the youth group on a bike ride around town and end at IHOP restaurant on Pine Street for breakfast. I made a few discoveries that chilly morning while riding a tandem cycle with Mr. Tommy. First, Ocala had many steep hills. Second, I was more of a social kind of youth group gal, opting for singing Amy Grant songs in the comfort of an air-conditioned chapel. I had not properly trained for a 10-mile ride.

From the back bike seat, I yelled to Mr. Tommy that I wasn't feeling well and could we possibly hail a cab. He encouraged me to use both feet while pedaling. Then Miss Pat breezily cycled past us with her typical big grin. She was always kidding me.

"Come on, Amy!" she yelled while laughing, "Don't you want to eat a big pile of pancakes right now?"

I'm not proud of this moment, but I believe I said something to the effect of while I appreciated her spiritual leadership, I wasn't ready to meet Jesus just yet. This is the same woman who took all the kids to see the movie "Jaws" at the beach. No wonder we spent the next day holed up in the hotel.

Brenda Adolf didn't try to kill or scare me, but she could have made me a recluse.

The minute I walked into the Adolf home, I never wanted to leave. She and her husband, Pete, a talented building contractor, had built a multi-leveled house near horse country. It was a lived-in kind of home with spacious rooms that offered oversized couches, comfy beds and a kitchen that always smelled of baked cookies.

Her daughter Wendy and I spent hours holed up at the house listening to Billy Joel and The Cars, working on Anchor and Little Women service club projects and dreaming about our future boyfriends, most of whom would never become our boyfriends and would be shocked they were on the list. Brenda always checked in on us with something delicious from the oven.

Brenda had the most ethereal countenance. Her kindness was radiation grade. I eventually discovered this was her secret weapon.

She could calm a crowd or naughty teenager with one soulful tilt of her head and knowing eyes. I never wanted to disappoint her. Time and again I saw how giving she was - to a fault, I suspect. She would give anyone anything. I hesitated to tell her that I liked something in the home décor store she owned because she would give it me! "Here honey, just take it!"

Through the years, we would run into each other at the grocery store, but my last connection with Brenda was her Christmas card with a personalized message she always included in her iconic beautiful handwriting.

Back to the mom box. Pat and Brenda have made me think differently about what kind of legacy I'd like to leave. Could I be in a mom box to my children's friends now who are young adults?

I hope I will always be a safe place to land in troubled and good times. I hope my home is open for comfort, dreaming and freshly baked cookies or a really fantastic Betty Cake.

I'll never be one to cycle 10 miles, but I'd drive 1,000 miles to see Bailey accept her journalism award or watch Alia graduate from college or see Allie's new workplace in Atlanta. These kids have become my kids. And Weston. And Julia. And Louie. And Will. And many more, Lord willing.

Any box will do. That's what Pat and Brenda knew and lived every day of their exceptional time on this earth. And they were spectacular at it.

Thank you, moms. I'll love you both forever.

Gold Star Material

One in the morning is probably not the best time to make a major life decision pertaining to your child's education. Lucid thoughts are clouded with fatigue and by fingers stuck together from a hot glue gun. Yet, amidst the piles of construction cutouts and unused foam boards, I've come to a conclusion about class projects—each family member should be graded.

I arrived at this observation after an exhaustive marathon project-fest in which my husband, son, daughter, and I were consecutively working on two major class assignments with an imminent deadline, meaning the next day. Emotions were raw, tempers flared. Then, the Popsicle stick ship collapsed under the pressure of too much glitter. It looked like Barbie at Plymouth's Rock.

The boys weren't doing any better. The craft paper wouldn't adhere to the shoebox frame of the Iroquois longhouse. They dismissed my suggestion to say this was a post-hurricane longhouse. Heated words were exchanged and time-out was enforced with the kids separating my husband and me in different rooms.

Other parents have suffered through similar experiences. I know this because I see them, circles under their eyes, carefully delivering their cardboard projects to the classrooms. As if this isn't bad enough, we have to compete with the projects worthy of Harvard University. It's tough when your kid's toilet paper roll Eiffel Tower is placed next to an architectural rendering of the Palace of Versailles that would make King Louis XIV proud.

I speak from personal experience. I am a survivor of the 8th grade science fair.

My project correlated the Rorschach Psychological Inkblot Test to gender. I had a cow's brain in a jar, which had no relevance whatsoever to the study, but it caught everyone's attention. Always the marketing major, I had a logo on my exhibit with a matching shirt that read, "As The Mind Turns!" Never the biology major, I was stumped when the judges asked for clarification between genetic disposition and neurological conditioning. "Hmmmm, that's a good question. Do you like my shirt?" It didn't help that I was next to the student who had discovered a cure for kidney infections. Okay, great. But where's your clever logo, honey? She nailed the question-and-answer time with the judges. I readjusted my cow brains. I could've used some help from mom and dad.

Since I've been on both sides of this equation, I'd like to offer some observations and a recommendation. First, here are a few tips for creating a successful class project:

· *Glue guns are king. Buy them in bulk.*
· *Ditto on poster boards.*
· *Toothpicks provide limited structural support.*
· *Volcano replicas are so yesterday.*
· *Most importantly, craft stores close at 9pm and the clerks get really nasty when you bang on the door.*

So, I humbly submit this recommendation to teachers—require the following questionnaire be completed by the parents:

· *Did you assist your child in the development of this project?*
· *Were you able to complement your skills with that of your child's?*
· *Did everyone share in the responsibilities?*
· *Most of all, did you have fun working on this together? Will you heed my call for parents to rise and unite? It's time for a revolution! Let us lay our midnight burdens down. We shall come together and demand a curriculum overhaul!*

OK, perhaps that's a stretch. Can we get a gold star sticker? Did you at least like my shirt? ❄

Triumph of the Turtle Parent

My youngest child graduates from high school this week. In a few days, I will sit on a crowded bleacher watching robed graduates receive diplomas. They'll also receive words of wisdom via the obligatory commencement speeches about new chapters, rites of passages and journeys. Usually a poignant story is thrown in for good measure.

Students have spent years dreaming of this moment. Parents have spent years bracing for it.

Thus, I'd like to offer a commencement speech for parents. Mind you, very little of this speech is original. But this isn't my first rodeo as a parent of a graduate, and I simply want to share some insight I've discovered along the way. I'll also try to avoid the word "journey," but no promises.

Here goes.

To the Parents of the Graduating Class of 2015 (and any other class), congratulations! You helped your child grow into a young adult. You navigated the rough waters of insecurity, angst, disappointment and rebellion. But enough about you.

Your child faced some pretty stiff challenges, too: high school testing, college entrance exams, social acceptance, dating, not dating, thinking about dating, more testing, Snapchat. It's a lot for you both. You had to learn how to parent in a teen's strange world of pervasive social media, and your child learned (hopefully) the virtue of patience while showing you multiple times how to save documents in a computer cloud.

But here's the good news: You did it. And now for some advice.

First, get some rest. Take a post-graduation nap. You'll need it. You're not done parenting. If anything, you've just begun. Now comes the hard part — parenting a young adult ready to leave the nest and establish some independence from you.

Sometimes that space will feel like the distance between the earth and the moon. It can be gut-wrenching. Other days, the distance will narrow in scope and tone. Out of the blue, your son will call for advice. Your daughter will send you a text of gratitude, maybe even suggest a visit. It's as if the universe is securely back on its axis. But it will shift again because that's what growing up is all about, ebbing and flowing.

So rest up. Get healthy. You are ebbing and flowing, too.

Often we speak of life as anecdotal chapters of a book. But life is sometimes more realized in paragraph form. We change jobs, college majors, life partners, friendships, interests, passions. For some, the story is abbreviated. This time last year, I celebrated the graduation of a close friend's high school graduate. Today, my friend – a dad in his 50s — is gone, passing unexpectedly this past winter.

So my next piece of advice is this: Work on your narrative today.

You've probably lived much of your life nurturing your child's story that I bet yours got buried. Dig it up. Don't wait. Don't second guess either. Just as you have told your child that life has many twists and turns, so does yours. Go after something you've always wanted, even if you change direction down the road. No time like the present. I believe one of the best parent-adult child relationships are those in which parents have their own life stories, their own identities that naturally intertwine with family but are not entangled in it.

Oh, and this is really important: Have fun. Goodness knows, you've had plenty of worry and stress as a parent. To some degree, that never goes away, it just changes. Go out with friends you couldn't see because the babysitter fell through. Join a book/dinner/anything club. Spend time with people you've always wanted to know better. Spend time with yourself also.

I think of Frances, a great-grandmother who decided to go to college when she was 78 years old. She took a humanities course I taught. She not only set the grading curve, but also inspired her classmates — younger by decades — with her unbridled enthusiasm.

"I'm having a blast and that's all that matters," Frances once told me. "I decided I could either sit at home waiting for the grandkids to visit or go out and have some fun and sit in a college classroom."

This is not to say that parenting doesn't possess pure joy and fulfillment. It does. Big time. But you are now at a point you can create some of your own happiness in addition to and apart from that of your child's. So get out there!

It is turtle hatching season on our Florida beaches (cue the poignant story part of the speech). Their entry into our world amazes me. The mother turtle lays eggs in the deep soft beach sand then heads back into the ocean. The hatchlings break free from their shells. They are phototactic so they are guided by the brightest light, which is why they usually appear at night, drawn toward the moonlight. Local hotels put filters on their outdoor lights so the hatchlings aren't misdirected and end up in swimming pools.

I must admit I'd be the mother turtle hiding in the dune waving the hatchlings toward the sea, yelling, "Look out! Turn the other way! Avoid danger! Pack a warm coat!" Yet that's not how it works. The mother turtle has already done her part. Maybe she's taking a long nap on a quiet reef.

Somehow, miraculously, many of the hatchlings make it safely to sea. They find their way. And we will, too.

Congratulations, parents of graduates. You've got your hatchlings this far. Well done and well wishes for the life in front of you. ❄

Car Line

*M*y heart aches a little this time of year. The back-to-school promotions make me melancholy for days when I was checking off the school supply list for my children as they lobbied for their favorite lunch totes.

There's a social media video of a mom frantically rushing through Target while counting the reasons she can't wait to send her kids to school. I admit it's hilarious, but it doesn't quite resonate with me. As a young mom, I always found myself counting down the days until summer.

Yet, once the school year was upon us, I jumped in with maternal gusto, signing up to help with class parties, festivals and field trips. I coordinated school drop-off and pick-ups with other parents in our neighborhood. Early dismissal from school — better known as "half days" — were highlighted on my master family calendar for advance planning around work. And I couldn't leave out the ever-important gift schedule for birthday parties and holidays — trick or treat bags for Halloween, Valentine's in February and end-of-school teacher gifts.

By the time the calendar was complete, it rivaled a corporate project management spreadsheet.

I'm tired just remembering this flurry, making me wonder how the heck I managed it all? This must be why the young have young kids. The distance between sentimental memory and reality was often delicate juggling between work, home, school, sports and everything else.

For me, the best part about school was picking up the kids in the afternoon.

Sweaty and excited, my son and daughter would pile into our minivan's back seat and start non-stop talking about their day. I gleaned more in that

10-minute drive from Eighth Street Elementary to our house than a whole week elsewhere. By the time I pulled into the garage, I had the download on history homework (good), math test (ugh) and the presidential fitness test (excellent! A reminder that they were really more my athletic husband's children than mine). Most importantly, I read between the lines of what wasn't said — the pause after sharing who made the spelling bee, who sat next to whom at lunch, who got invited to that popular kid's birthday party and who didn't (son of a biscuit!).

Today, I drive solo in my compact car, sometimes ending up past the elementary school, remembering car line where the school's principal, the late, great Helen Ingrao, would shout on her microphone headset the names of students to get in the right car. "Tim, get in the car, hon! We don't have all day!" Then she'd walk up to my van.

"Hey, Mama," she'd say in her famous southern drawl. "Boy, it's hot outside today. Don't forget we have a PTA meeting on Thursday."

She'd hustle Grif and Gilly into the van, shut the door and tap it for my signal to keep the line moving. She was the original industrial engineer. She was also our leader when we celebrated the school's historic renovation project that commanded nothing short of a day-long celebration with a building dedication, ribbon cutting with community leaders and full-blown parade in the front of the school.

She died several months later, too soon and unexpected. I still have a necklace she gave to me for co-chairing the celebration.

Sometimes, in the early evening as the moss-covered oaks draw long shadows on the road, I drive through "car line" past Eighth Street, devoid of minivans and children and school staff directing traffic. And I think about what I'd give to have a backseat full of kiddos recounting their innocent days.

To the parents of school-aged children, I wish for you a blissful year of class parties and field trips. Be mindful of those moments in the car. Take it all in and be present — like turn-off-your-cellphone present — because, one day, you will probably find yourself driving past your children's school wondering what that mist is in your eye. ❄

A Twilight Mom Unmasked

*I*mmediately, I felt old and ill-attired.

Formal evening wear isn't your typical dress for a leisurely Friday night at the bookstore. Then again, the midnight release of Stephenie Meyer's "Breaking Dawn" was anything but typical.

And I was anything but young.

With an odd mix of trepidation, excitement and caffeine, I went to the unveiling of Meyer's final installment of her popular "Twilight" saga. The vampire romance has captured the hearts of post-Harry Potter fans and people who really like to dress up like werewolves and vampires painted in pasty make-up with blood-red lipstick. They talk in clipped, breathy sentences when ordering a venti double latte, soy decaf, while flirting with an extremely patient cafe server.

Prom dresses were everywhere. Bella, the story's central love interest of vampire hottie Edward Cullen, has a pivotal scene at her prom in the first book. So, crinoline-, silk- and glitter-adorned young girls lined the crowded aisles yelling, "I love Edward more!" "No, you don't; I love him more!" Then, they'd giggle and run off to the cafe for a chai refill and more flirting with the increasingly less patient cafe server who started checking his watch.

Not exactly the place you'd expect a mother of two who values sleep.

So why was I there?

You see, I'm a closet "Twilight" fan, a borderline groupie. This is a story of romance. I love romance. Vampires? Not so much, but stay with me. This is my confession: I was hooked at the very first paragraph, where Bella faces impending death. Then enters Edward, then Jacob. Oh, so many choices. Ain't love grand?

So, here I am in a Barnes and Noble on a Friday night, dragging my friend Kelly into this odd-yet-inspiring pool of literary teens and, like me, a few mothers masking their genuine interest in this most unusual love triangle.

I invited Kelly, suggesting we throw caution and our Target shopping list to the wind and do something bold — like stay up past 10 p.m. Our husbands and kids opted out — with a faint detection of snickering under their breaths — so it would be two middle-aged mamas out on the town.

Look out, Paris! The old girls were going to shake things up a bit!

OK, it was just a book release party. In Ocala. With teenagers. And one now-tense cafe attendant. Yet, as she's done so many — and probably regrettably — times with me before, Kelly signed on. The next step: pre-midnight party prepping.

We both took afternoon naps.

By 10:30 that night, we were dressed and ready. So were most of the area's young adult population who looked way more awake than Kelly and I, but we weren't going to let a little finely aged metabolism hinder our fun.

First, we checked out the book's trivia contest and decided that, since I had read only two of the books and Kelly none, we'd decorate masks at the craft table. Two new friends — Katelyn and Amanda, ages 12 and 13 — shared ideas on the series' ending, saying Edward was "totally amazing" and they "hoped Bella would marry him instead of Jacob."

Kelly pulled out her reading glasses so she could see where to glue her sequin. I asked our young friends if their moms had read the series since — ahem — there's a growing number of adult women catching the vampire fervor, or so I'd heard.

"Nooooo," they both replied in high-pitched unison. "Our moms totally don't get it."

Kelly and I nodded, "Yeah, ours either."

Just before midnight, we joined the book line behind a few Goth prom queens and a mature-looking woman about my age who was wearing a custom-made Bella bracelet with wooden wolf and crystal heart pendants. Wearing a "Cullen 01" baseball shirt, she said the series gave her hope for romance, adding the book has "done wonders" for her friend's marriage, too.

Dr. Phil needn't be worried. This isn't Jane Austen by any stretch. Yet, I have to admit Edward and Bella's smoldering romance is enough to keep the female reader's interest regardless of age or bone density.

For me, the journey began on a rainy summer day.

I decided to see what all the "Twilight" hype was about, and 24 hours later, I'd finished book one and was onto the second. Dare I say it? It was love at first bite.

I'm not into the vampire literary genre, although the love story works because of Edward's "I-can't-have-you-because-I'll-consume-you" dilemma. (Translated: lots of intense hand-holding and hugging. Kind of like Mr. Darcy Meets Dracula.)

Plus, Edward is just so darn sensitive. He caters to Bella's every whim — well, almost. He actually likes to watch her sleep. What's not to love? Hey, I read my share of serious lit, but when it comes to fun and fantasy, bring on the hunky vampire!

By 12:30 a.m., my caffeine high was waning, so with my new book in hand, Kelly and I headed home, joining the herd of prom queens and vampires migrating, nose-in-book, toward the parking lot. Surprisingly, my husband was still awake, mainly out of curiosity about my big night and to make sure I got home safely. Alas, here was my Edward.

The fact that he waited up for me was the best part of the evening — like, totally amazing.

I giggled all the way to my kitchen coffee pot to set the timer for morning. Then it was off to bed, where I would sleep like Bella until the dawn would break for the next new glimmer of "Twilight." ❄

Amy's very abbreviated summary of the Twilight series

"Twilight": Bella, the new girl in town, meets Edward, the handsome and sensitive vampire. First kiss is worth the book alone.

"New Moon": Time, distance and a nasty paper cut separate Bella and Edward. Enter Jacob, Bella's new best friend who just happens to be a werewolf. Maybe Bella needs to take a break from boys.

"Eclipse": Bella is in serious danger and must choose between Edward or Jacob. Hmmmm — werewolf or vampire? Either way, it can't be good. Still more heavy hand-holding.

"Breaking Dawn": No spoiler here: Is immortality highly overrated? Will Bella marry sun-averse Edward or move on, graduate and get a high-tech job at Microsoft in Seattle?

Livin' It Right

We live in paradoxical times and I'm not referring to our current political season. I'm thinking more of John Mayer. This gifted guitarist and singer has often connected with the mercurial essence of being a young adult. His song "Why, Georgia" contemplates the restlessness of it all living in one's 20s, a sentiment relevant today, commonly referred to as a quarter-life crisis.

"Am I living it right?" Mayer asks. As the mother of two young adults who is also close to many of their friends, I have a front-row seat in the theater of youthful emotional exegesis. They feel pressure to figure it all out. Yet, isn't this the time in their lives when they don't have to?

I passed quarter-life a long time ago. I can't even say I'm at the mid-life point anymore unless there's been an uptick in women living to the age of 102. So, I'd like to think this affords me the vantage point of been-there, done-that. To the quarter-lifers, here's what I know:

First, feeling insecure about your life and becoming an adult isn't a crisis, it's a gift. Without sounding all Oprah, we are fortunate at any age when we have the ability to fret about what's next. But, it's a balance, too. Worry can keep you from moving forward, not to mention enjoying the here and now.

Second, you will never have it all figured out. Ever. Give yourself permission to explore. I say this a lot to my quarter-life friends who are transitioning from college, overwhelmed by what to do, especially career-wise. Repeat after me: This is all good. You have choices. Pick one or two and don't look back. Which leads me to this...

You will have a lot of firsts. And some lasts. Love. Jobs. Friendships. Apartments. Unused gym memberships. Learn from them. Go to the gym more often. And don't stop loving because a relationship didn't work out the way you'd hoped. My desk calendar has inspirational quotes; last month's was "Here's to a year of making all the right mistakes."

Fourth, college can be contradictory. On the one hand, you have many academic options. On the other, you've got to pick an area of study and stick with it or suffer the wrath of an undeclared major. It's all right. You may not end up in the right major. You can change it. And, if you can't, that's OK, too. Use your undergraduate experience in creative ways. Your major may not be your life's vocation, but it can be an unexpected springboard to something else.

Fifth, please, please limit your exposure to social media. I'm serious. Instagram, Snapchat, Facebook and Twitter feed the fire of youthful insecurity. It also keeps you from living. Nothing replaces real-life relationships and real-time experiences. Bear with me as I know I sound old here, but you'll look back and wish you had taken more lunches and trips and long walks with friends and family. And gym workouts.

And finally, slow down. I know you have an elevated sense of urgency and an enviable metabolism. Soak it all in. Try not to let some falsely imposed alarm clock limit a really special time in your life before mortgages and daycare enter into the picture.

This is the month of college acceptance letters. To the young adults who are getting the college welcome notices, congratulations. Here's to making all the right mistakes. You will make some wrong ones, too. You'll be just fine.

And aren't you lucky.

Packing Up A Life

The glorious days of spring are here, which means three things in my world: clear blue skies, honeysuckle in full bloom, and moving at least one of my offspring. As another college semester winds down, the packing tape comes out. If I had a dollar for each time I've moved my children, I'd have enough to, well, buy more moving boxes.

This month's move is bittersweet — my youngest graduates from college. Once again, I find myself wondering where the time went. Seems like just yesterday I was loading up her orange and blue totes into my car while holding back tears realizing my baby girl was about to leave our nest. Now, she's moving home as a Gator grad, but, alas, her stay is temporary. In August, Mike and I will move her to an out-of-state graduate school.

My son has also moved again, this time into his own place and is taking his bedroom furniture from our home. This includes the twin beds he's slept on since a toddler that previously belonged to Mike when he was a young boy. You'd think I'd have this moving gig down pat, and, in many ways I do. However, I find myself unpacking emotional memories with each move. It's like the "Groundhog Day" movie, only I wake up every day misty-eyed thinking how my young adults are adulting so seamlessly.

Since most parents practice this same rite of passage, I'm offering some suggestions how to best manage moving kids to college. They'll hear enough wise words at graduation ceremonies. I doubt commencement speakers include moving tips, so here are mine:

Moving Tip #1: Be a planner. Make a list of what must be moved, when, where and how. Load up coat hangers, cleaning supplies, totes and trash

bags, the latter which can be used for moving clothes on hangers in bulk, a trick I learned from my sisters, who are also veteran parent movers.

Moving Tip #2: Be economical. As Mike often says with each move, "Remember, what you move up, you have to move back." Limit your Target run to must haves, not wanna haves, except for decorative white lights on a string. I think it's a requirement all college freshman rooms be adorned with little white lights.

Moving Tip #3: Be flexible. The first time I moved our son to college, I was in awe of the controlled chaos outside the dorm. Know this: there is never enough parking space for unloading stuff, so be patient and listen to some cool music as you drive around the campus for an hour until it's your turn.

Moving Tip #4: Be hydrated. In dead-of-summer heat, bring plenty of water as you walk up and down five flights of stairs because all freshmen must live on the highest floor of any residential building. It's a rule right up there with the little white lights.

Moving Tip #5: Be restrained. There are many things you'll want to say to your child as you stand outside your car getting ready to leave. Don't say them. Rather, write them down, then meditate over them with a prayer of gratitude. You have the chance to watch your child spread his or her wings, then say only this, "You're going to do great. Inhale every moment. Have fun and study hard. I love you."

Moving Tip #6: Be gone. Know when to leave. No sense hanging around embarrassing yourself, although I did threaten to cling to my son's legs yelling, "Don't go!" Instead, I collapsed my sweaty self into the car and slept the entire three hours back home without waking and, as my husband said, more importantly, without taking a bathroom break. It was my own little miracle of grace for this emotional mama sorely in need of one.

HERE AND NOW

Prelude for a Princess

My goodness. Has it really been 20 years since Diana, Princess of Wales, died? The end of this month marks a somber anniversary of the Paris car crash that claimed her life. Diana would have turned 56 last week. I remember both dates, just as I remember she loved forget-me-not flowers, went through a polka dot fashion phase and listened to Rachmaninoff while writing notes at her desk in Kensington Palace.

Like many of Diana's contemporaries, I was fascinated from the moment "Shy Di" timidly appeared on the palace steps with Prince Charles announcing their engagement.

We were three years apart in age. I was a 16-year-old riding the mercurial teenage life of a high schooler while surviving the requisite bad hair perm and futile teenage romances. Diana was 20, titled at birth, and engaged to the most eligible bachelor in the world. We had little in common. Yet, I was hooked. I subscribed to *Majesty* magazine and created a Royal Family library in my apartment.

Regrettably, I once got the signature Princess haircut without the signature Princess's thick hair and, well, face. The perm didn't help.

Through the years, I recruited other HRH Princess of Wales fans, namely, my friend Mary, who swapped British magazines and books with me as we enjoyed scones and a hot cup of Lady Londonderry tea, Diana's favorite. We squealed on the phone when another Diana event was publicized — the time she danced with John Travolta at the White House, rode a water park flume with her young sons and cut up with Sarah Ferguson, the Duchess of York, at polo matches. Just your typical, run-of-the-mill royal stuff.

Until it wasn't typical anymore. Things got real, even for the princess. Actually, her life was always quite real. She bore the emotional scars as the daughter of bitterly divorced parents and an estranged mother. She suffered depression. She was bulimic. And, as we now know all too well, her marriage was irreparably broken, almost right from the start.

Yes, Princess Diana was charismatic, compassionate, fun loving and beautiful. But she was also scorned, disillusioned, insecure, judgmental and impetuous. She was vulnerable.

In other words, she was human.

And with her humanness, she became even more interesting to me. The last year of her life was the most revealing. There she was on the other side of a public and humiliating divorce. She dated around, worked out at the gym and dove into passions that fueled her, namely advocating for the most sick and wounded. She hadn't quite figured out that self-care is self-love and that no other person, not even a prince or heart surgeon or a rich man with a yacht, could make her whole.

Given more time, I'd like to believe she would have come to this realization if not for stepping into a black Mercedes near midnight on Aug. 31, 1997.

She was this close to liberation.

Maybe that's why she loved Rachmaninoff's "Piano Concerto No. 2 in C," and why wouldn't she? This piece was her music doppelganger. Soft then fierce, ending with a thunderous orchestral climax, the composition rolls and ebbs like the life of a heartsick yet hopeful woman in the prime of her life. A title could not entitle Diana with a contented life. She was no more immune to hurt and disappointment any more than the rest of us.

But her struggle and triumphs were for all to see.

A few years ago, I donated my Diana books and magazines to the public library. Holding on to them felt surprisingly bittersweet and dated, seeing images of a life that wasn't all that it seemed. I much prefer to recall the post-royal life Diana was creating without a script.

In one of her last interviews before her death, Princess Diana said she wanted to be remembered as "Queen of the people's heart." No doubt she has been.

To me, however, I'll remember her as someone who was on the path of reclaiming her own heart, the truest part of her being. A legacy that is not reserved to only royalty.

The Perils of Planning

wo bouts of the flu landed me in an unplanned and protracted period of time in bed. Not the way to ring in a new decade.

After a few days piled beneath the covers watching Nancy Meyers movies (trust me, they are good for what ails you), I decided to live again and walk into the living room. There I saw a pile of magazines, some colored ink markers, tape, and an 8 ½ x 11 foam core board, exactly where I left them pre-sickness. Ah, yes, the makings of my annual vision board.

Many years ago, my friend Diana introduced me to her New Year's Day tradition of creating a poster where your current dreams and goals come alive. No rules to this, she'd say, just write out your BHAGs — big hairy audacious goals — find or draw images that give you inspiration and promise to place your dreams-on-a-poster somewhere you'll see it every day.

Keep in mind, this came way before The Secret or Oprah's Soul Sunday. She was on to something. Now there are YouTube vision board tutorials.

I haven't kept up with this ritual on a regular basis, but when I do, lo and behold, I seem to accomplish more things. I also tend to overestimate how much I can get done in a year.

My early vision boards were chock full of dreams, some big, some small. Through the years, I've scaled back to a more attainable list. Or at least I thought I had.

Back in early December, I bought a new work planner. The front of the planner is dedicated to listing annual goals, details for each goal and key actions to accomplish those goals. This thing even breaks every goal into daily and hourly accountability steps as well as a weekly reflection on what worked, what didn't.

Like a good planning soldier, I filled in every single line and page. Some days, filling out the planner was so much work, I woke up an hour early just to complete it. This is progress, right?

As New Year's Eve approached, it was time to transfer my dreams from the planner onto the vision board. Reviewing the list, I felt queasy. I would need help in order to meet these goals, as in another human or two. As in these goals were not humanly possible.

Now, several weeks later, I realize it was the planner that made me sick! Excessive goal planning had infiltrated the drinking water in my house. All of the action steps, workday rituals, focus details and details about the focus details had literally infected me. Someone should alert the Centers for Disease Control and Prevention; this could be an epidemic.

When my fever subsided, so did my desire to bring down the industrial-day planner complex. Instead, I took a deep breath and checked myself before I over-planned myself. Now with fresh eyes, I worked on my vision board with a simplified scale of dreams. My BHAGs are few and not so big or audacious, but meaningful to me.

This year, I'm striving for attainable over audacious. I'm feeling better already.

How to Survive the Coming Recession

Ten years after the Great Recession, my family and I are still living with the fallout. We lost our jobs, home, health and, for a short time, I lost my emotional sanity. While life has gotten somewhat better, I've developed an acute case of the gimlet eye toward the future. I'm a worrier by nature. Some people do CrossFit. I fret. The country's financial collapse was like gasoline on fire, leaving me permanently scarred. Yet, looking in the rearview mirror of the crash, I try to use my experience as a lesson for what lies ahead. And there is always something that lies ahead. As the wise philosopher Yogi Berra once said, "It's deja vu all over again."

Nothing lasts forever according to divorce lawyers and economists. Even white-hot economies overheat. It's not a matter of if, but, when another recession hits. Here are 11 ways to prepare for when it does.

Be a Pessimist. It'll Do You Good. Once the eternal optimist, I made a career choice based on hope, passion and Oprah. I thought living my best self meant leaving a stable job to become a magazine editor. It was the heady bull stock market of 2005 when I gave up a tenured college teaching job with health insurance, a pension and summers off to be with my children to write about homes and gardens. Here was my Optimistic Mathematical Formula for Living: Everyone was living in spectacular homes and gardens. I loved to write. I loved home decorating and writing about homes and gardens. I, too, could live in and write about spectacular homes and gardens and get paid for it. Therefore, I was living my best life! Yay for me! Enter 2008. Buh-bye, Mr. Bull. That year wiped out my job, checkbook and best life chakra. Belief in unfunded dreams is something you have to recover from. Sure, life can be a drag if you go around thinking the worst is going to happen. However, as one speaking from painful personal experience, isn't it better when you're pleasantly surprised?

Remember: Your Day Job and Passion Aren't an Either/Or, But a Both/ And. In case you were totally bummed by Tip #1, take heart: you can have your cake and eat it, too. You just have to make sure you can afford the ingredients. My husband had the misfortune of working for a major brokerage firm that severed ties with thousands of employees three months after I lost my job. Two weeks before Christmas. With no severance package. My editorial job was gone and so was my husband's. We thought we had been bold and brave in our choices to start new careers that promised good fortune in intangible and tangible ways. Now we were unemployed and uncertain about our future and that of our children's. Ten years later, we both have steady jobs while my writing career is doing quite well. I have a newly-published book that is resonating with readers. Turns out they've led reinvented lives, too. Does this mean I'll pursue a full-time writing career? Not a chance. I'm keeping my day job. Honestly? I could win the lottery and you'll find me at my office the next day.

Heed Your Personal Warning Signs. In the course of ten years, we had moved six times, my husband and I lost three jobs, my son and daughter were diagnosed with life-altering chronic health conditions requiring daily, sometimes hourly, medical care, my father and mother-in-law died and my mom had a stroke that sent her from her home to an expensive assisted living facility (is there any other kind?). Oh yeah, and the American economy collapsed. My dog died, too. Those who knew of my situation would say to me, "You are so strong!" I wondered. Did I have an option? For a long time, I didn't think I did. That's when I asked for help, both professionally and from family and friends. Actively solicit support. Don't struggle alone. Shouldering the burden of stress is unsustainable. You ain't Hercules. When the next recession hits, you'll be fortified.

Save For a Rainy Year, Not Day. This one is pretty straightforward. Save. Then save some more. Repeat. I had three months of savings and minimal debt when the recession hit. It wasn't enough. Shoot for a year. Better to overestimate what you need. I'm not kidding. Those cafe lattes and Netflix subscriptions aren't worth it. Trust me.

Shun the Shame. I'm channeling my inner Disney movie when I say to let it go! Of the guilt you're not where you thought you'd be professionally, romantically or personally. Of the shame you can't hang with those who spend more in a day than you do in a month (hint: they're probably more in debt than you). Of financial embarrassment because you can't afford your child's field trip or girls night out. You can help out the teacher in return for the field trip. And cosmos are so yesterday. Truth? Life isn't picture perfect like Instagram. Remember that shame is a paralyzing kidnapper of your soul. And pride is a close cousin. Let go of someone else's perception of success. Embrace your own.

Chocolate Helps. So does meditation and a nice walk outside. In combination, all three contribute to living a healthy, balanced life. Take time to get in mental and physical shape. Coping mechanisms don't develop overnight. Work your core now.

Dancing Helps, Too. I decided to ascribe to a saying I once saw on a cocktail napkin, "Trust me, you can dance. Love, vodka." In the darkest time of my life, I chose to dance. Who cares if I was Tangoing in my 800-square-foot apartment's kitchen that was the size of my former closet? I was moving instead of constantly sitting in front of my computer completing job applications. Take well-earned breaks. Good enough is good enough. And Tony Bennett is better than Xanax.

Grudges Never Help. Work on your capacity to forgive and forget while you can still pay your bills. For a long time, I held a long-term grudge match with a financial corporate entity who was responsible for my husband's job loss. Many companies were tone deaf to the realities in which most of their employees worked and lived. Yet, I encouraged my children not to keep grudges. Do as I say not as I do, right? Keeping score is a metastasized anger that leaves little hope for an emotional cure, I'd tell them, but I was beginning to realize I had fallen into the do-as-I-say-not-as-I-do category. It wasn't so much that I harbored ill will toward those who had hurt or disappointed me in some way, real or perceived. I learned to move on. But, hurt my husband? My kids? The deal was off.

I loved the story from Rabbi Marc Gellman who showed children in his temple a hands-on demonstration of grudge-holding and forgiveness. He hammered nails into a board and told them to think of each nail as a bad thing someone does to another person. With each pounding, the kids got upset. Then he pulled out the nails, asking his young audience to think of that as what happens when we say we're sorry for each bad thing we've done. The children smiled, realizing there is something they could do to make things right. Then he showed them the board with all the nail holes in it. How to get rid of the holes? They had no idea. He admitted he didn't either. The holes would always be there.

I was trying to hammer fewer holes. I kept the grudge tool kit away from view and tried to remember where I had put my compassion supplies, but sometimes I forgot. It was easier to grimace and grudge. Since then, I've tried to do better, fret less and judge little. I've lost my appetite for such pettiness, both in others and in me. I've stopped obsessing about who knows what about my situation. Who cares? They have holes of their own, often irreparable voids from a tragedy or illness or loss of some kind. I got over them and myself.

Home is Wherever You Are. I'm going a little Yoda on you. Home you are, I say. Sure, stuff is nice. The ultra-suede sectional. The 3400-square-foot Cape Cod escape. Sub-Zero refrigerators. My wake-up call came in far too many emergency rooms for my children. Those Sub-Z's didn't matter so much. Stuff is stuff. Radical life perspectives can be a gift. Start now in prioritizing how badly you really need what you think you really need.

Pay Attention. Focus on the GDP not TMZ. Federal forecasting can be spotty. Do your homework. Stay informed. Read the economic tea leaves by following legit business-oriented media. Ten years ago, I didn't know the difference between a tranche and a trench. Now I do and hope to avoid both.

How rich is the irony that I was once a home and garden editor without a home. Life is a lot like a remodeling project. We are all renovated. Repairs are necessary, sometimes requiring a complete overhaul. When the next recession arrives, I will be ready. Will you? ❖

 Learn from Failures and Bears

A long time ago, I was on a search committee for a new hire at work. Our interview panel used an agreed-upon list of questions for the top three candidates.

One of the questions consisted of what I call "The Miss America" prompt: "What is a weakness that you have?" Now, if this were a pageant, the reply might have been, "My weakness is that I'm a perfectionist and only want the best for others and the world." But this was a job interview and two of the three candidates gave a satisfactory answer. Yet the third candidate's response is one I've always remembered, decades later.

He said, "My weakness is I have a tendency to make mistakes and not learn from them."

You could have heard a pin drop.

The candidate went on to explain. He gave a few examples to illustrate ways he fell short of success. Not delegating assignments to other teammates. Failure to ask enough questions at the front end of a project. Lack of time management. Repeatedly. He was so specific citing his weaknesses that I wanted to ask him to stop talking before he dug himself deeper into the black hole of bad interview answers.

Then he finished by adding, and I'm paraphrasing, "But I have come a long way in recognizing this vulnerability. And I'm working on it. I have researched the team I would work with if you choose me for this position. They are a team of strong and diverse leaders. I could learn from them. Of course, I also believe I have skills I can bring to your company. But I believe an important part of growing as a leader is possessing the ability to recognize areas of improvement. Look, I've worked for teams who didn't know this and the results had long-term negative repercussions."

This reminds me of the saying, "What doesn't kill you makes you stronger. Except for bears. Bears will kill you."

Not to dismiss the importance of possessing and developing strengths as part of one's core character, but you can learn a lot from failure. I sure have. Like the job interviewee, I've made some mistakes a few times before I learned from them. Eventually, I stopped tripping myself up and moved in a different direction. However, I first had to recognize the pattern.

So much of our culture emphasizes not only what we do well, but also what we do well with gusto. The political candidate who answers with definitive soundbites. The student who doesn't hesitate when answering a question. The co-worker who jumps in to take the lead on a project.

Often, these actions are interpreted as strengths. And sometimes they are. But, sometimes, we would be better served if we paused. Did our homework. Added some self-reflection if we were up to the task. Were honest about our shortcomings.

Certitude can work both ways, both leading and limiting. Weaknesses, if analyzed thoughtfully, can inspire perseverance. I don't stop striving to get better; however, I've found that taking time to swim in the shallow end of my failures has made me a better, stronger swimmer for life's deep end.

We hired the candid interviewee for the job. Eventually, we both moved on to different jobs, but I saw him last year at a meeting. He is now a senior leader in a large organization, widely respected for his work with others. He is probably still failing on some level, but I bet he remains open to what that can do for him. ❖

Wired on the Now

*I*n this dangerous, stressful world, cowering beneath a rock isn't the solution, though I bet it's cool and quiet there.

Caring for family members who suffer with chronic conditions, I've learned the value of managing stress. Most recently, I was with a doctor who offered sage advice not only for his patient, my daughter, but also for the rest of us.

"Block out the things you can't control," he said. "There are a lot of troubling events in the world right now, don't carry it all."

Wise words. Now if it were only that easy.

I say this as a veteran worrier who carries burdens like a champion weightlifter, often crashing beneath the pressure from an overpowering barbell of concern. Age, experience and necessity have lessened my load for the good, but that's usually during the hours I'm sleeping. Separating the real stress factors from the imposed is a skill. You practically have to wear blinders to ignore the deluge of stomach-turning events in our country and world.

Try anyway.

I know people who are naturally wired for information. They are on top of the latest news article and social media feed to stay current and connected. I'm no better or worse, subscribing to a couple of newspapers each day and satellite radio news channels. But, out of sanity preservation, I have consciously decided to pick and choose what I absorb and what I don't. Kind of like the serenity prayer, though I'm still working on that wisdom-to-know-the-difference part. Let me get back to you on that one.

Cowering beneath a rock isn't the solution, though I bet it's cool and quiet there. All things in moderation, right?

That's what my daughter's doctor was suggesting: Take in only what you can manage and discard the rest.

I've discovered the beauty of seasons. Not fall, spring, winter or the eternal Florida summer, but the emotional kind. Sometimes, there is a season to respond and become engaged. Other times, it is best to stay exactly where you are for the moment and just be.

A friend once told me that, when it comes to responding to stress, she started small. One bite of the pie at a time (using a food metaphor calms me already). What's the one thing I can do at this moment? There's usually something. Maybe it's a call to someone who can help. Or researching a solution online. Or, in my case, sitting on a hospital bed with my daughter playing Name That Tune to the melodic off-key songs that kind of, sort of sound familiar if only they were sung by Beyoncé. I couldn't change where we were, but I could adjust the stress volume down a notch with a riveting "All The Single Ladies."

I've also come to respect the prospect of hope over what's hurting. Cue my daughter. One of her college friends, Bailey, texted a picture of a "goals board" she made out of framed paint chips (trust me, it's adorable). Using markers on the glass frame, Bailey sketched out her dreams for the life she'd like to have. A few days after leaving her latest hospital visit, my daughter Gilly decided she would make one, too. I loved it so much I made one.

Forget about goals, our creations were really about hope. Because, in the words of our doctor, that is the one thing we can focus on. ❄

The Eulogy of You

I t's been a week of extraordinary eulogies. Between the funeral services for Aretha Franklin and Sen. John McCain, I've logged quite a few hours watching tributes.

What struck me with both memorials was the intimacy. After hearing the solemn and celebratory homages, I felt as though I knew Franklin and McCain so well that they could have stopped by my house for dinner or at least an afternoon adult beverage. Such is the beauty of well-written and spoken praise.

When the daily newspaper arrives, some people do crosswords, I read obituaries. Every. Single. One.

While I don't know most of the people who have, in the words of poet John Gillespie McGee, Jr., crossed the surly bonds of earth, I connect in a surreal way. She loved time spent with her family, especially making quilts for each of the grandchildren. He never missed a football game with his children. She helped the homeless with her advocacy and fundraising. He retired as a military officer. She enjoyed spending time with her book club.

As I read each love letter to those who have passed, I think, yes, a life well lived. Followed by, what would I want to be said about me?

Once, I participated in a writer's workshop that asked this exact question. What would your eulogy be? I thought the workshop would primarily be writing about our childhood and favorite puppy, so I recalibrated to pause on this jarring question. To get the writing flow going, a few eager beavers volunteered to share their responses. It was nothing short of an emotional purge. Hardly any of the writers could read their first sentence without crying.

Want to get to the core of what your life should be while you're still living? Write your eulogy.

This experience was so moving that I decided everyone should write their memorial tribute while living. Do this while you are fresh and young and hungry for the next chapter — assuming there will be a next chapter. To understate, it is a humbling exercise to write what you want to be known for. Here is what I discovered in the process.

Everyone loves a story. The hero's journey never gets old. Flawed, scared, wounded, you've lived it, so tell it. The more real you are, the more connected you will be. Tell the story that you thought didn't matter. Tell the story you wish you would have known when you were able. Tell the story that just might have saved you from unintended consequences. When you tried to reach a goal only to have fallen. That's the hero's journey, after all.

For the record, I loved the small, seemingly inconsequential stories of John McCain. The passing conversations in the hallway, the encouragement he shared to fellow colleagues. His story of intently standing six inches from George W. Bush's face before a presidential debate commanding him, in one simple word, to "Relax!"

Everyone loves connection. Whether we want to hear this or not, we are more connected than we are different. We are loved. We have succeeded. We have failed.

Everyone will have an obituary. Hard though it may be, this is the universal truth of life. We will live and we will die. What will we do when we are here on this precious earth?

Write that.

Still, I think we have it backwards. Eulogies should be given while we are still alive. While I doubt this will become a trend, maybe the best thing to do is live the life you want to be written about.

After all, isn't that the best tribute of all? ❊

Busy Doesn't Live Here

have a habit shared by a few million others right now: wishing away a period of time.

For me, this involves dreaming of the day after something I must do that (a) is stressful or (b) might be mundane, but necessary or (c) involves a treadmill. In the case of said million others, there seems to be a desire for tomorrow to be the day after the presidential election. I get it. We're nearing the saturation point of ugly accusations, innuendoes and threats — and I'm just talking about Facebook posts.

But, I'm trying to change my fast-forwarding mindset. Here's why: It is not helping.

Hostile election seasons aside, I've decided to make the most of each day; unoriginal, I know, yet, awfully hard to do.

I blame Apple and whoever invented Outlook. First, my phone is constantly pinging me reminders of things I must do. Sure, I can modify my notification prompts, but they're still there, those minute-by-minute calendar items taunting me and whispering in my ear, "Amy, just because you swipe 'clear' on an event doesn't make it go away." Such a know-it-all, my smartphone.

The real blame, of course, falls on me, the feeble master of my scheduling destiny.

We live in a culture of "busy," or, as some lament, "crazy busy," which, translated, means a life chock full of things to do. And it appears there is no down time. Here's the thing: I don't do crazy busy. At this stage, I've perfected the antidote to crazy busy: crazy napping. But, life has gotten so hectic lately that I find myself looking forward to that elusive down time.

Often, it's a weekend with no scheduled plans or a holiday in which serious snoozing can occur.

Here is where I fall into the Wish-Away Trap. I start wishing away my busy days, anxious to get beyond them.

"This time next week, I'll have that project done," or "If I can get to Friday, I can relax." My favorite Play It Forward, however, is the most maternal one: "In just four weeks, I'll have all of my family under my roof together on college break."

Which brings me to the elections.

Increasingly, the collective sentiment is the desire to hunker down and pray for post-election daylight. Yet, another Wish Away. To all of you feeling the same way, I offer my humble attempt to resolve this plight with one simple action: Want Today Instead of Wish for Tomorrow.

The wise poet Garth Brooks sang that we must be mindful if tomorrow never comes, so let's make sure we have few regrets. Hence, I've begun prioritizing activities into my calendar that should be on the top, not the bottom, of the proverbial To Do list. My time blocks are quite straightforward with titles such as "Family" "Fun" and, even the once-dreaded "Health Hour" that involves walking with friends whom I never get to see.

Suddenly, I love exercising! Walking and talking? I'm in!

But, what to do for the next two weeks?

A good start would be to step away from clicking on social media or television. Dial into actually being with someone or something you care about. This doesn't mean you have to shun the political process. Quite the opposite. This election cycle, I've heard a lot of voters talk about social causes, and you know what? Those causes still need help — the homeless shelters, the Title I schools, indigent health care. Show up. You'll make a difference. Each day. Not tomorrow or the week after.

Only one thing is certain: I have this moment right in front of me. I want to make it count. ❁

SMILE

Love Letters for Short People

n eighth grade, I had two goals: grow taller and date a boy who was in my science class. The odds were against me. Delayed puberty would keep me from reaching five feet for another year. Middle school's social hierarchy prevented me from obtaining lifelong happiness with Science Class Boy.

He was in the cool, athletic, popular clique and won all the gym class awards. I won a trip to the school nurse's office for throwing up after running relays on field day. You try running with a short gait, I told the coach.

Yet youth is often blessed with blind optimism. On Valentine's Day, I prepared a declaration of my affection in a hand-written note. My best friend Tina was also in the class and agreed to proof it. I had no intention of giving it to him. Writing sappy notes was half the fun. I poured my emotions on thick with this one — it would have made Jerry Maguire proud. Science Boy completed me. I drew hearts around his name and mine.

Enter obstacles three and four: Rachel and Robby. Rachel was the known gatekeeper between the popular group and the rest of us. No one could talk to the clique without going through Rachel. She was the consiglieri of eighth grade. Robby was the class trouble-maker whom students feared and teachers loathed.

Both were in my science class.

Sitting at my desk, I pulled the love letter from my notebook to pass to Tina sitting two seats ahead. Rachel sat in front of me, and normally didn't acknowledge my existence, passing my notes to Tina as if she were swatting a fly. Not that day. Maybe it was my sense of urgency that tipped her off. Science Boy was sitting in the row beside her and I had no margin for note passing error. Rachel held my note as Tina awaited the hand-off. However, she paused, revealing a sly smile and began reading the note. Just as I went to grab it from her, someone tapped me on my shoulder. It was Robby, who sat behind me.

"Hey, I got this for you," he said, handing me an unwrapped 45 rpm single record. It was "Short People" by Randy Newman.

While I was momentarily distracted by Robby, Rachel did the very thing that consiglieres do — she capitalized on another person's vulnerability. She gave my note to Science Boy.

My stomach soured, like I was running a relay.

The teacher turned around from the chalkboard. All I could do was sit frozen at my desk contemplating a move to another school as Science Boy read my letter.

I did not transfer schools. I survived the Note Passing Crisis of Eighth Grade, though Science Boy and I never dated. He would smile at me when we passed in the hallway, but I didn't want his pity. He's turned out to be a nice adult. Rachel, too. Kind of. Tina is a really good high school teacher. And Robby? A well-regarded furniture designer. Go figure.

After school that day, Tina and I walked to my house where we played Robby's gift on my record player. That's when we noticed he had written a note on the record's paper jacket.

"Happy Valentines Day. I saw this and thought of you. I think you are nice."

Troublemaker had a crush on the short girl. I'd like to believe he did not listen to the song before giving it to me. "Short people got no reason to live ..." Really?

No matter. I eventually grew taller. And wiser, leading me to meet my husband who makes me feel like I could touch the stars on any given day. Even Valentine's. ❈

A Green Jacket to Remember

hen I think of The Masters Golf Tournament, I think of egg salad. Not your usual gloopy store-bought kind. I'm talking about a homemade creamy mustard-mayo combo with delicate chunks of hard-boiled eggs between two pieces of soft, melt-in-your-mouth white sandwich bread, no crust. The tournament, held at Augusta National, invites local high schools to host food trucks where they make and sell a ton of egg salad and pimento cheese sandwiches.

Twenty years ago this weekend, I went to The Masters. It was a trip to remember, and I'm not even a golfer. I don't really care for eggs, either. But the tournament and the food made for a once-in-a-lifetime experience.

The greats were there — Arnold Palmer, Jack Nicklaus, Gary Player — and they made room for some new young greats on the leaderboard — Phil Mickelson, Ernie Els and a young player named Tiger who would win it all that Sunday, his first of four coveted green jackets.

And to think I almost didn't go.

I had a five-month-old baby and two-year-old. The thought of leaving them didn't thrill me, nor the effort of actually dressing in something besides a T-shirt and sweatpants, the outfit of choice endorsed by most young moms decades before yoga pants.

Ya gotta go, my husband said when he found out he and his good friend won four tournament passes in a charity fundraiser. Uh-huh. I'm not leaving my babies and I can't fit into any of my pre-pregnancy clothes. Then buy new outfits, he said. Take a friend, I said. Trust me, he said leaning in for dramatic effect, you will regret not going.

So I went. I'm glad I convinced my husband to take me.

The tournament was everything sportscaster Jim Nantz said it was. An exquisite landscaped course so vividly in technicolor and crisply manicured it looked like God himself painted it with a big green crayon and meticulously trimmed each blade of grass with surgical scissors.

The arriving fans, fervently clasping their prized entry badges like it was Willy Wonka's golden ticket, respectfully moved through the clubhouse gates at an almost solemn pace quietly nodding to each other. Hello. Yes, we made it.

We're on hallowed ground. Shhhh. Act like you belong here. Remember, not a peep when the players are about to swing or putt or walk by or breathe near us. Utter nothing. NOTHING.

The crowd swarmed near Tiger so we went elsewhere. Up and down the hilly fairway we walked. And walked. And walked.

That's when the hunger set in.

Enter egg salad.

I'm not sure if the sandwich was that good (it was) or I had fallen into a sensory stupor (I had) from the Crayola-green course and the electric pulse of celebrity golfers passing by and the unspoken, but acknowledged, feeling of being alive and present at one of the world's greatest sporting events on one of the world's greatest courses.

Probably all of the above. Totally worth those dozen egg salad sandwiches I consumed (sad, but, true.)

As the sun set each day, the mowing brigade arrived, sweeping across the course in perfect synchronized unison as the masses exited as humbly as they entered, ready to rest and restore before the next round of impeccable play, pristine setting and egg salad.

Come this weekend, I'll be glued to the television set, grateful for the commercial-restricted policy only The Masters can command. I'll pull out the scrapbook our friends made for us after we returned from Augusta. They were the other lucky couple winning the golden ticket to golf's mothership. Flipping the pages, I see a boyish Phil Mickelson as he leans into his putt. And Fred Couples shyly smiling at the crowd. There we are, Mike and me, wearing golf visors with the iconic Masters logo.

And Tiger. Lots of photos of the young phenom.

I witnessed Tiger revolutionize a new season of golf. He was alive, electric. Twenty years later, turns out he was kind of just like us — human, flawed. Now, he's ready for a comeback.

Will this be his year? Doesn't really matter to me. He's still here. And so are we. Ready for another tournament of a lifetime. ❋

A Reckoning Like No Other

t began with this year's Miami-Florida football game. I was out of town for a board retreat and the scheduling universe was not aligning for me to watch the most hyped match for an opening game. My Gator buddy and UF alumna daughter was eight hours away as a graduate student in Birmingham trying to find a sports channel that showed anything other than Alabama or Auburn. And my Gator-fan husband? He was the lucky one donning orange and blue at Camping World Stadium ready for kickoff. Two out of three Mangan Gators were feeling out of sorts.

Adding insult to injury was the fact that an FSU graduate was the board's CEO, responsible for the retreat's calendar date. The game never entered her mind, she said! Of course it didn't. Good thing she's an exceptional human being and leader and we love her anyway in spite of her collegiate alliance. Our Seminole friend made things right by her Hurricane and Gator board members and rearranged the agenda while securing optimal viewing with a few flat screens at a hotel bar. Worked for me!

Meanwhile, back in Nick Saban land, Gilly connected with another Ocalan expat to watch the game in the privacy and safety of her friend's apartment. In Orlando, Mike was doing the Chomp at the 40-yard-line, 10 rows up. And in a small coastal village from both child and husband, I was nervously sipping an adult beverage watching pre-game pundits predict their winner.

Okay, we were set. Well, not quite.

I was still feeling a little off without my football La Familia. Then some friends in Gator attire pulled up two chairs beside me. Gil and L.T. were excited. In the past year, we three became close through our involvement with the organization whom we had traveled to support. Two-and-half emotion-filled hours later, we had formed a bond like no other.

By the third quarter, things were looking bad for my team. I mean ugly bad. Too many self-inflicted defensive pass interference wounds were shoring up to be what looked like an imminent Miami victory. Gil, L.T. and I yelled, cheered, yelled, and cried a little more at the TV screen. A commercial break gave us a respite.

Then it happened.

L.T., an apparent optimist and soothsayer, channeled his inner prophetic intuition and uttered seven words that have now become legend. He turned to Gil and me and with a big smile and said, "We are about to have a reckoning."

I thought this was the bourbon talking. What say you, oh Gator oracle?

Methodically, L.T. led us through his prediction for what would happen after the commercial. The Gators special teams will get a fumbled punt return from the Canes. This will give us short field advantage. We will score a touchdown and take the lead. We will continue our good fortune in the fourth quarter and will win by 3 or 4 points.

"It will be the reckoning," L.T. emphatically proclaimed.

And that's exactly what happened. As in that is exactly what happened. Every play L.T. predicted came true. Miami couldn't score in spite of the penalty-and-interception-prone Gators. Each time, Gil and I would look at each other, shrug our shoulders in beautiful disbelief and shout "It's the reckoning!"

After a rousing "We are the Boys of Old Florida" fourth quarter tradition, I sent a group text to Gil, L.T. Gilly, Mike and our mutual friend Derek, who was with Mike at the game.

"IT'S THE RECKONING!" I texted to which everyone would respond, "BRING ON THE RECKONING!" We exchanged photos of ourselves with incredulous looks reminiscent of Edvard Munch's "The Scream."

Since that night, this same group opens up a text before each Gator game. And each time, I'll be darned if there isn't another Gator reckoning that one of us predicts – Kentucky, Tennessee, Auburn, South Carolina, LSU. Okay, strike that last one.

I've even called a few reckonings. Gil is my witness. He and his wife were with us in Ocala watching the Kentucky game. We texted Derek, Mike, and L.T. throughout. Yes, Mike was sitting next to me on the couch, but we couldn't break a good streak.

We'll need some major reckonings for the remainder of the season. Georgia's up next, then Vanderbilt, Missouri and FSU. Should we get to December heading to Atlanta, rest assured there will be some mighty reckoning banter burning up the cellphone.

Sure, it's just a game. And the Gators are just a team. But, our "Reckoning Crew?" Well, they're something special. My prediction is we will be Gator La Familia for a very long time. ❈

From Casserole to Cassoulet

rowing up in a Southern family, I came to appreciate the diversity of a casserole. We had one for every occasion—egg casserole for breakfast, hot chicken salad casserole for lunch, and hamburger casserole for dinner (green bean casserole an alternative on Saturday nights). This was an equal access recipe—we welcomed all ingredients into the mix. Naturally, my cooking expertise was founded upon this inventive concept of meal-in-a-dish.

For a long time, the running joke among my family and friends was that I could make a mean squash casserole, and, upon closer inspection, you could detect the yellow vegetable buried deeply beneath a pile of saltine crackers, sour cream, and melted cheddar cheese. (Paprika is optional if you want to get all fancy like you were from Georgia or something.)

As a newly engaged bride-to-be, some of my colleagues at work presented me with a bridal cake made of squash casserole, complete with a plastic bride and groom on top. My future husband looked worried.

As the years progressed, so did the Mangans' waistlines. Something had to give. The word "cholesterol" was uttered by my Northern-bred doctor who actually said he had never tasted a squash casserole. And to think I took serious medical counsel from this man. Get thee to a diner and quickly! Throw in some peanut butter pie while we're at it! Still, he wasn't budging. My hips were, however.

After surveying my kitchen pantry, I could see some gaps in the nutritional scheme of things. Maybe three cans of shortening were a bit excessive. And I could probably find a way to exclude fried onion crunchies from most meals. Some would even go as far as to say cream of mushroom soup could be considered optional when creating a dish. I didn't want to appear to be rash, however.

So, I focused on culling through my cookbooks. Many had to go, but it seemed wrong to discard the church's recipe collection by its members. Now, there was a group of individuals who understood the virtue of starch. A church picnic was simply incomplete without a Tater Tot casserole. Still, I knew I needed to broaden my Epicurean horizons, though not necessarily through my thighs.

Seeing the quandary I was in, my friend Mary introduced me to the works of Ina Garten, the popular American chef known as the Barefoot Contessa. At first, I was hesitant to try Garten's French-inspired recipes. Just the thought of French cooking made me nervous. I didn't know a croissant from a cracker. Easing gently into the world of truffles and Julia Child, I watched Ina's show on the Food Network. She made it look so easy. And she looked like she was having fun. And she served wine. This can't be all bad. Plus, the food looked delicious.

Next thing I knew, I was making a salad out of tomato, mozzarella, basil, and olive oil. Goodbye, Thousand Island dressing, hello, fresh herbs! No saltine crackers for me! I served brioche! Viva La France!

Then it dawned on me—the real joy isn't in the food itself. Happiness—at least for this converted Southern cook—is derived more from the idea of preparing the food for someone and with someone. Ina taught me that, but so, too, did my mother, grandmother, and sisters frying up a good chicken while mulling over each other's lives. That's better than any formal recipe I know.

Yet, I have to admit, I've grown in terms of culinary expertise. I puree my squash now, honey.

Bon appetit, y'all.

Ill Advised

A scratchy throat is the first sign. Masking as a nagging tickle, my throat now throbs with pain each time I swallow. I know what comes next. By morning, I will have a full-fledged head cold. Yet, in spite of this knowledge about the sequence of symptoms I will inevitably develop, I insist upon following a complex pattern of diagnosis and treatment on the off chance the outcome might be different than, say, the previous seven other times I had a cold.

Stage One—Spousal Assistance. Moaning loudly and frequently usually gets my husband's attention, but not for long. Rushing into the room while holding his breath, he hands me a cup of hot water with lemon (What? No codeine?) and tells me to get some rest. Luckily for him, my throat hurts too badly for me to verbalize a response, so I make distinct hand gestures instead.

Stage Two—Sibling Intervention. Next, I call my sisters who, although not formally trained in pharmaceutical studies, possess an impressive and extensive vocabulary of recommended prescriptions. "You need some Erythro," says Julie. "Or maybe a Z-Pak," adds Cindy (we like to abbreviate our antibiotics like they do on Grey's Anatomy). Both agree I am in dire need of Codeine. I love my sisters.

Stage Three—Maternal Guidance. A child can never be too old to call her mother who quickly assesses my situation and offers some antibiotics that have been in her refrigerator for the past six months. She thinks she might have some cough syrup with codeine in her pantry if she can find it. I love my mother.

Stage Four—Surgical Contemplation. One of my friends tells me about an acquaintance who had a sore throat and needed emergency surgery to remove polyps the size of golf balls. Certain of my prognosis, I call the doctor and inform her receptionist that I've cleared my calendar for the rest of the week in anticipation for the throatectomy I'll need (Dr. McDreamy did the procedure once, so I know it works.) My husband checks in to see if I drank the cup of hot water yet. No, Dr. Jeremiah Johnson, I've been a little busy adjusting my I.V. pole of fluids to stay hydrated.

Stage Five—Children Interruptus. Sleeping upright prevents further nose drippage until my children tap firmly on my shoulders. They said Dad sent them to find out what I was fixing for dinner. I suggest that, since their father is so talented at creating hot beverages with lemons, he considers making something for the children to eat. Then I give them the cup of water, telling them Dad would know exactly what I'd like for him to do with it.

Stage Six—Medical Prognosis. Finally, I see my doctor who twice rescheduled my appointment. Personally, I think the patient with the appendectomy was overreacting. An appendix is optional, a throat is essential. After doing a rather cursory examination, the doctor scrawls some notes on her pad and wishes me well. I look down. She recommends use of a saline nasal spray three times a day, bed rest, and hot water with lemons. Clearly, my husband got to her.

Immediately, I drive to my sister's house where my mother is waiting with The Pill Book to analyze additional options. If all else fails, I'll gulp down the dadgum cup of hot water with lemons.

Just don't tell my husband. ❄

❧ Well-Seasoned Memories ❧

M y relationship with food is a lot like my dependency on books. I can't go too long without either one. Sometimes, this leads to excess, an explanation, in part, for the five extra pounds I gained while reading Pat Conroy's Prince of Tides. Who knew an entire bag of Hershey's miniature chocolate bars has more calories than one regular-sized bar? The blame, however, belongs to Conroy. If he had shortened the book by a couple hundred pages, his protagonist Tom Wingo could have spared himself the emotional damage of his childhood and I could still fit into my jeans.

This flawed logic has followed me for many years. I'm a nibbler. I can't get through a chapter in a book without grabbing a cherry-licorice Twizzler. Pretzel sticks are good, too, but dipping them in peanut butter results in sticky fingers and even stickier pages, a distraction but not an impediment. I struggle to remember my Social Security number, but can quote, word for word, a verse from the Wendell Berry book I read six years ago and the jelly beans that accompanied it (Toasted Marshmallow and Very Cherry Jelly Bellys, in case you were wondering).

My enthusiasm for food goes beyond the literary spectrum and, well, just nibbling, too. Special times, events, and places are etched in memory laced with carbs and, usually, lots of them. Like the trip to Charleston Mike and I made 13 years ago when I was six months pregnant with our first child. We visited historic sites, shopped for antiques, and walked along the waterfront. What historic sites, you ask? Hmmm. I'll get back to you on that. But, let me tell you about the crème brûlée at Slightly North of Broad Restaurant. Pure heaven. I've craved that caramelized custard ever since.

The lightly-breaded chicken medallions in brown sauce at The Moon and Sixpence in Bath, England, also come to mind. What Roman baths? Sorry. I was too busy licking my fork. I do remember the water, though. It was next to the soft, warm bread roll and creamy butter.

A friend once asked me to recommend some places to see while visiting San Francisco, a favorite spot I used to frequent before children and theme parks came into my world. I reminisced about the homemade coconut macaroons at the Petite Auberge Inn and Zuni Café's mouth-watering ricotta gnocchi. And you can't go to San Francisco without having a milk chocolate caramel or two at Ghirardelli Chocolate on Fisherman's Wharf—it has a killer view of that big red bridge whose name escapes me. Just kidding. It was dark chocolate, not milk.

The writer Nora Ephron said, "I have made a lot of mistakes falling in love, and regretted most of them, but never the potatoes that went with them." I would add to that my mom's macaroni and cheese—the kind with mounds of sharp cheddar cheese, elbow pasta, and dollops of salted butter—that got me through many a heartache. Or my family friend Josephine's shrimp Pad Thai and clear noodle spring rolls when I was pregnant and on bed rest. And I'll always remember the out-of-this-world pecan ice cream and crêpes my friend Cynthia made when Gillian was born.

Life is seasoned with the memories we make and, in my case, the pasta I eat. I'm getting hungry. I think I'll take a break and read a bit.

Now, where did I put those Twizzlers?

Dance Lessons

friend once told me her superpower was dancing in heels. Mine would be dancing in Spanx. In spite of a constrictive undergarment, I'm fairly nimble on the dance floor, a feat I discovered while taking dance lessons.

It began with my husband's Christmas present to me, a month of lessons with a trained instructor, meaning someone full of more grace and patience than the Dalai Lama. When we arrived for our first lesson, I was like a newly announced candidate for the American presidency, full of optimism and well-pressed attire. An hour later, I was a wrinkled figment of myself, limping to the car while recounting triple and rock steps.

Yet, hope springs eternal, so hubby and I returned for a second lesson. And a third. Then a fourth. We're regulars now, high-fiving our fellow students as we enter the dance studio, mildly shocked we keep showing up. We're limping less by the end of each lesson, instead skipping to the parking lot shouting energized goodbyes to classmates.

A few surprises as a result. First, I underestimated the power of togetherness. Sure, dancing is a great bonding time with my husband, but it has also given me a chance to grow new friendships with fellow dancers. None of us are professional twinkle toes and this strengthens our resolve even more. We celebrate each other's dance steps just as quickly as we laugh off a failed one. Or two. Or three. When we switch partners, we immediately apologize for any lapse of recall on the routine sequence. Absolution granted.

I'm also pleasantly surprised I've learned two different dances in a short time period. This, coming from the woman who once kept re-entering her home address incorrectly into an online application until permanently blocked. My mental synapses may not correctly fire, but muscle memory glides muy fantastico to the Salsa.

And I'm humbled by the fact my marriage has remained intact. I am sure there are moments on the dance floor that my husband is thinking, "Why didn't I just buy her a bookstore gift card?" We do our best to resist the familiar tug of marital behavior, but old habits die hard. I dance with the intensity of a sledgehammer. He moves more quietly with a steady pace as if to say, "Surely, the old gal will tire soon." But, he doesn't give up and neither do I. Together, we interpret the choreography of a partnership that has outlasted the hokey pokey and, blessedly, the Cupid Shuffle.

Not every lesson is easy. Sometimes, it's tempting to stay home. After a long day of work and life, I consider my options of slouching on the couch watching "Dancing with the Stars." Instead, I rally, finding my place beneath the disco ball.

It's a stretch to consider dancing in public outside the comfort of the studio, but I'm willing to give it a try. Whether with my dance classmates or husband practicing the East Coast Swing, I'm happy to move to the music while it's still playing. ❖

I'd Like to Thank Pinot Grigio

*A*llison Janney pulled a humility twist this past Sunday night. Upon winning the Oscar® for Best Supporting Actress, she held the golden statue and said, "I did it all by myself." Then she smiled, acknowledging nothing was further from the truth.

Isn't that great? For a moment, she said what no one else would: "I worked hard for this and, while many supported me through the hard times, ultimately, I made a choice to get up every single day and put my big girl pants on."

There's a balance between acknowledging the help of others and admitting that no one pushes you better than you.

No one made Allison try for audition after audition, rejection after rejection. No one said, "Oh, Allison, you'll win the Oscar one day, wear a rockin' red gown and all those hurtful reviews will be worth it." Of course, she had friends and family and coworkers who believed in her. She said as much in her acceptance speech.

Which got me thinking. What if we wrote our own acceptance speeches for pivotal times in our lives? What would that look like? Here are a few thoughts:

The early years acceptance speech: To my kindergarten teacher, I'd like to thank you for not choosing me to be the star actor in our class play. You taught me the virtue of resilience. Who wants to be a bunny when you can be a skunk? That's what my mother told me when I came home crying the day you announced your acting choices.

"But, honey, the audience was laughing with you," Dad said after the play as I pulled off my skunk ears in the backseat of the car. In the spirit of Allison Janney, I'd like to thank my five-year-old self for not succumbing to stage nerves and mortification while singing, "I'm a little stinker and I might stink you."

The teenage years acceptance speech: Let's face it, a 15-year-old's life is ripe with killer speech material, but I can pare it down to two words: Air Supply. I owe this music duo's "All Out of Love" and a driving sense of self-preservation for getting me through many a heartbreak. Copious amounts of Oreo cookies and mint chocolate ice cream also helped.

I'm-in-my-30s acceptance speech: Thank you, Loonette, the famed clown of "The Big Comfy Couch" children's show. You transfixed my children with your visits to Clowntown so this young mom could make breakfast and get ready for the day. You also gave me permission to accept the dust bunnies beneath my couch. I will always love you for this.

I made it to the midlife acceptance speech: Thank you, Pinot Grigio. That is all.

The wow acceptance speech: At this point, life is one big wow. Wow, I'm still here. Wow, wasn't I just 20 years old like a minute ago? Wow, when did my eyelids start to sag? Wow, who knew HGTV could be so deep? Watch "House Hunters" for a crash course in human psychology and you'll see. Wow, life is beautiful. Wow, life is hard. Wow, going to bed early really is a good idea. Wow, nothing beats love. Ever.

To members of the academy of life, thank you for the privilege of living it. I owe a lifetime supply of Oreo cookies in your honor. ❋

How Sweet is That?

*J*ames Taylor is making headlines. The voice behind iconic songs like "How Sweet It Is (To Be Loved By You)" and "You've Got A Friend" released a new album, "Before This World," earning his first No. 1 hit on the record charts. But, that's not what the buzz is about.

Taylor is trending because he accomplished this at 67 years old after a five-decade career in the music industry. Words like "remarkable" and "finally" are associated with his No. 1 spot as if this has been the brass ring Taylor has wanted all his life.

What I find more impressive is the fact he's been making really good music for over 47 years.

That's remarkable.

We get hung up on getting to that top spot whether it's on a Billboard chart, in an executive corner office or a graduation rank. Human nature drives competition — often fiercely — hitting the gas pedal to the floorboard toward some group's definition of success.

I partially blame social media that feeds ego like fuel on fire to get the most Likes on Facebook or hits on YouTube. Perhaps I'm just insecure. I still don't know how to do Instagram correctly.

I'm guilty, too. I like to see who has shared and commented on my Facebook dribble. Artists like Taylor are especially expected to perform well on many levels. Musicians and writers are scrutinized by the business side of their profession with high demand multi-leveled marketing campaigns.

I thought content was king. Twitter has become its heir.

Sure, it's great to strive for excellence. I admit I found it gratifying that Taylor bumped the other Taylor — as in 25-year-old Taylor Swift, for readers above age 20 — from her No. 1 song slot she has held since she was born playing her guitar in the delivery room. It seems that our definition of excellence has been narrowed to unrealistic expectations, rock star or not.

Our community got into the public discourse fray over a local high school's 27 valedictorians. I know many of them. They're brilliant, talented and giving. I thought the conversation was somewhat misdirected. Rather than focus on the merit of how many is too many who hold the top rank, why not also recognize other students for their unique achievements?

I think of some of my former college students who went to school full time while working and raising a family. And one who earned his two-year degree to work in the medical field in spite of severe test anxiety. They would tell you their satisfaction came from making their lives better for themselves and those whom they love.

Wouldn't that inspire others like them if they got a shout-out, too?

The senior-aged Taylor dismissed his chart-topping feat in a recent radio interview. He responded to the question of what the No. 1 hit meant to him. He said he just liked making music and felt he still had something to offer.

Yes.

Being number one as a sole motivator limits life's learning process. In my half century on this planet, I've realized how success can be subjective. I strive to do what I define as my best and it's not all bad when it clicks. It's OK when it doesn't, too. Life is more than a one-time win. There's also something to be said for living in the now as much yearning for the next rung on the ladder.

Taylor sings as much in his new album's title song how thin the moment is, ever so narrow.

And ever so lovely that Taylor has enriched our lives with song for most of his.

How sweet is that? ❊

Acknowledgments:

This book, this life would not be possible without the love and support of Mike, Griffin and Gilly. I began as a Yeary girl inspired by my parents, sisters and extended family. My cherished friends are an extraordinary gift. I'm immensely grateful one of them is Steve Codraro who has been my design muse and friend throughout my writing life. Special thanks, also, to editors and fellow writers — my ever-present champions — including one young and brilliant journalist, Bailey LeFever, who served as my book editor.

Thank you so much for reading one of Amy Mangan's books.
If you enjoyed the experience, please check out our
recommended title for your next great read!

This Side Up by Amy Mangan

"*This Side Up* will leave you feeling relieved, not alone, hopeful, and grateful for a friend and writer like Amy Mangan who inspires us to reframe our let downs, have some laughs, and embrace life with all of its beautiful unexpected messes."

–Stacy Strazis, former producer *The Oprah Winfrey Show* and *CNN*

View other Black Rose Writing titles at
www.blackrosewriting.com/books and use promo code
PRINT to receive a **20% discount** when purchasing.

CPSIA information can be obtained
at www.ICGtesting.com
Printed in the USA
BVHW090354311021
620274BV00005B/130